COLLINS WILDLIFE GARDENER

STEFAN BUCZACKI

COLLINS
WILDLIFE
GARDENER

STEFAN BUCZACKI

Collins

First published in 2007 by Collins
an imprint of HarperCollins Publishers
77-85 Fulham Palace Road
Hammersmith, London W6 8JB

www.collins.co.uk

Collins is a registered trademark of HarperCollins Publishers Ltd

11 10 09 08 07
6 5 4 3 2 1

A catalogue record for this book is available from the British Library.

Designed and produced by Airedale Publishing

For HarperCollins
Publishing Director: Denise Bates
Editor: Alastair Laing
Designer: Wolfgang Homola
Senior Production Controller: Chris Gurney

ISBN   978 0 00 723184 3

Colour reproduction by Colourscan, Singapore
Printed and bound by Printing Express Ltd, Hong Kong

Contents

WHAT IS WILDLIFE GARDENING?

In this section of the book I look at the origins of wildlife gardening and at the garden as an important habitat after the decline in areas of open countryside in Britain. The principles behind wildlife gardening – fostering and preserving native plant, animal and insect species and following environmentally friendly, and sometimes organic, practices in general – are also explained. Finally, I advise on ways to adapt your existing garden or use a virgin plot for the benefit of wildlife.

The expression 'wild life' (two words) first appeared in 1879, meaning 'the native fauna and flora of a particular region', unlike domestic animals and cultivated plants that live where they do because of the actions of humans. The word 'gardening' is as old as the hills. Such terms as 'flower gardening' and 'alpine gardening' are understood by all to mean the growing of particular types of plant.

Wildlife gardening is different in that it doesn't mean the growing of wild life, although it might, in part, embrace the growing of native plants. More importantly, and certainly here, it means gardening in such a way that the native flora and fauna are adversely affected as little as possible and, if at all feasible, are actively assisted and encouraged.

I don't see wildlife gardening, however, as an altruistic activity. All gardening should give pleasure to those who do it, and the wildlife benefit should be an additional consideration. If you want to be totally altruistic and helping wildlife is your only concern, then you aren't gardening but running a nature reserve: very worthy but not my topic here.

Below The field poppy (*Papaver rhoeas*) is perhaps the most popular wild flower.

Wildlife gardening pioneers

This isn't the first book about wildlife gardening. They have been around for 20 or so years but most are concerned with gardens that are planned and run almost entirely with wildlife in mind. In this book, though, I am just as concerned with those people who want a 'normal' garden and would like to take account of the needs of wildlife as far they are able, so long as it doesn't affect too greatly everything else in their plot.

There is a fairly long history of individual gardeners who recognised that their gardens had things in common with the countryside beyond. By far the most important was the Reverend Gilbert White during the 18th century (*see right*). Nonetheless, it wasn't until the late 19th century that another great naturalist, Charles Darwin, became the first person to use his garden and garden plants to test biological theories. He can't be described as a wildlife gardener in the sense that we understand it today for the simple reason that the environment wasn't then considered in any way threatened and in need of the support of sympathetic horticulture. That has come about only in the past 40 or 50 years, and I have always believed it began in 1962 with the book *Silent Spring* by the American author Rachel Carson. She was most concerned about the widespread and almost unregulated commercial use of chemical pesticides that persisted in the environment for many years with desperate consequences for certain wild creatures and plants. She drew the public's attention to the nature and meaning of food chains: how persistent chemicals absorbed by plants are absorbed into the bodies of animals that eat them, which then pass the noxious substances into predatory animals that feed on them, and so up the scale to end up in the 'top predators'.

Gilbert White

The Reverend Gilbert White was the Vicar of Selborne in Hampshire during the 18th century. He is famous primarily for his book *The Natural History and Antiquities of Selborne* (an original illustration for the book is shown above). First published in 1789, the book still makes absorbing reading. It was based on White's entries in his journals, and includes notes on his own horticultural activities. In addition – and this was what made the book new and pivotal – he wrote about the birds, insects and other creatures that lived in and around Selborne.

The decline of pesticides

Huge strides have since been made in limiting the use of persistent chemicals in commercial farming and horticulture. The response by legislators and commercial interests has filtered down to gardening where, year by year, the numbers of chemical pesticides available for use have steadily dwindled.

The decline has sometimes come about because of a straightforward recognition of the danger of pesticides' persistence or inherent toxicity and sometimes because newer and more stringent safety and testing procedures have resulted in them being uneconomic to produce. This has been reinforced by other environmental campaigns, such as preserving peat bogs by urging gardeners not to use peat-based composts. There is now also the wider recognition that we live on a threatened planet and it is incumbent on us all to take whatever measures we can to protect and conserve it.

The garden as a habitat

At its simplest, a habitat is the place where any animal or plant lives naturally – it's sometimes called its 'natural habitat'. Some creatures have gardens as one of their natural habitats, although there are few, if any, that have gardens as their only habitat – in other words, there are very few that never live anywhere else.

Even those creatures that have the word 'garden' as part of their common name, such as garden warbler, garden spider and garden centipede, certainly live in places other than gardens. As wildlife gardeners, we are trying to persuade creatures that our gardens are preferable to any of the other habitat options available to them, and the reason we are doing so is, as much as anything, because we enjoy their company.

Creature comforts

Hedgehogs (*Erinaceus europeaus*) are good examples of creatures that most people would like to welcome into their gardens. There's no great shortage of hedgehogs in the countryside at large, and a garden that attempts to mimic the countryside is unlikely to be especially appealing to them. In fact, what I call a dedicated wildlife garden (*see p.146*) is paradoxically not likely to be an especially good hedgehog habitat. By contrast, a 'normal' conventional garden with its vegetable plot and flower beds and relatively high slug population offers a much more attractive proposition – at least as far as a food source is concerned. What it may not do, though, is provide enough undisturbed places for hedgehogs to hide, breed or hibernate. It's here that a dedicated wildlife garden can complement the traditional plot.

Left The common garden spider thrives in gardens that attract flying insects, such as flies and wasps.

Above In the average garden there may not be enough hiding places for hedgehogs.

Some animals, such as frogs, have adapted precisely to the conditions in which they will thrive and need very precise habitats, while others have much vaguer demands. Overall, the degree to which animals are restricted in their natural habitats is simply a reflection of how catholic their needs are for food and shelter. Animals, such as hedgehogs, are undemanding generalists and will live in many different types of countryside, eating a wide variety of other creatures, and sheltering and hibernating wherever suitable conditions present themselves. In Britain, hedgehogs are only significantly absent from coniferous woodlands, moorland and extensive areas of cereal crops. This is partly because they may not find their preferred food there but perhaps, more importantly, because they prefer to shelter and hibernate among piles of fallen deciduous leaves, which are largely absent from such areas.

For more information about the garden as a wildlife habitat, try the following:

Garden Natural History, Stefan Buczacki (Collins, 2007)
The Natural History of Selborne, Gilbert White
  (many editions)
Biodiversity in Urban Gardens in Sheffield (BUGS) –
  www.bugs.group.shef.ac.uk

Left Woodpeckers depend on mature deciduous trees, where they nest and hunt for insects by drilling into the bark.
Below Frogs may lurk beneath water lily pads in wait for their prey.

Woodpeckers, by contrast, are never far from the old deciduous trees that they need for their food and nest sites – if your garden doesn't offer these, woodpeckers will be less likely to visit you, unless you are crafty enough to provide something artificial, such as food on your bird table, that appeals to them because it's easier to obtain than their natural diet of insects.

Other creatures are even more demanding in their choice of habitat. Frogs and toads, for example, may occur among damp vegetation considerable distances from any ponds or streams, provided they can find enough food, but they will be unable to breed there because their eggs or spawn must be laid in water. In addition, tadpoles (their juvenile stages) are entirely aquatic. For the same reasons, frogs and toads may visit your garden but will be unable to breed there unless you have a pond.

Plants that grow anywhere

The examples I have given above are of truly wild animals that we might want or hope to see in our gardens but comparable habitat considerations apply to plants, too, and should always be borne in mind when we are selecting species to grow – either for wildlife or 'conventional' gardening motives.

Some plants, native and exotic, will grow almost anywhere. Among the native plants that occur practically throughout the British Isles is creeping buttercup (*Ranunculus repens*). It is very undemanding in its habitat needs, which explains why it grows naturally in many gardens as a weed. If you wanted to grow it in your wildlife garden, you would be bound to succeed, wherever you lived. Another plant with, surprisingly, a comparably wide distribution is an introduced species: pineapple weed (*Matricaria*

Above *Calluna vulgaris* and most other heathers are acid-loving plants that will not grow in alkaline soils.

discoidea). Originally from North America and eastern Asia, it has adapted readily to the wide range of habitats in Britain. Clearly there was no native species that already occupied the habitat niche it needed and no other species seems to have suffered from its colonisation of Britain. It, too, will grow in any wildlife garden. I have it in mine, as birds feed on its seedheads, it's small and interesting, and, despite its astonishing success at colonising much of the British Isles, it's not an aggressive plant or difficult to keep within bounds.

Plants with specific habitat needs

Other plants are more exacting in their habitat needs. The heather *Calluna vulgaris*, for example, is one of a kind known as calcifuges, which are intolerant of alkaline soil. So if you want heather in your garden, either in its natural form or as one of the many cultivated varieties derived from it, you must offer an acidic soil. Plant habitat considerations are sometimes extremely precise. Water lilies, for example, need water, and you won't have any success with them if you don't

have a water garden. But some water lilies have even more detailed needs: not all thrive in all depths of water, few enjoy running water, and none benefits from the constant spray of a garden fountain.

Accepting a garden's limitations

No wildlife-friendly garden can attract or cater for every kind of wild plant and animal. You need to recognise the limitations imposed by where you live and how much space you have to replicate nature. But you must also recognise the limitations imposed by the very fact that it is a garden. Unlike natural habitats, a garden is entirely artificial – it is something you have created. It contains plants that you will never find growing together naturally, and it is affected by what you do to it season by season, such as collecting fruit, digging up vegetables, planting bulbs, filling containers and so on. Even if you have an area devoted to native plants and to attracting wildlife that looks like a natural field or wood, it won't really be one. It's a replica, a stage set, but there's nothing wrong with that. We can still all do a huge amount to garden in a wildlife-friendly way – but don't set your ambitions and expectations of re-creating the countryside too high.

A genuine natural habitat has taken years, possibly hundreds or thousands of years, to arrive at its present state. In a wood or on a river bank or cliff top, animals and plants of many different kinds have arrived at a fairly stable equilibrium. Through competition and adaptation, the habitat has developed to provide sufficient food and space for certain numbers of certain species. Other species may in times past have grown or lived there but have been unable to compete effectively and so have left, usually without trace. Barring some catastrophic event, like a flood or fire, the habitat will change little and then only slowly. If we want to create a little wood, a water-side habitat or a rock garden, we don't have hundreds of years in which to do it – but by closely observing what real habitats look like and understanding how they arrived at their present appearance, we can make a pretty good attempt.

Plants or weeds, animals or pests?

The notion that all native plants are weeds is well rooted in our gardening psyche, yet growing beautiful native species is the principal object of many gardeners' labours. To some, particularly vegetable growers, animals and insects are pests, to others they are welcome visitors. So where does the wildlife gardener stand?

Wildlife gardening, just like natural history, can be approached from two standpoints – in terms of the overall habitat or in terms of individual plants and animals. I shall be discussing the role of exotic plants in wildlife gardening later but the plants of our own countryside will always be especially important. Are these plants beautiful native species or are they weeds? It's useful to understand just where the differences lie.

There are many definitions of weed, some facetious and fanciful – 'a plant growing in the wrong place' and so on. *The Oxford English Dictionary* rather grandly offers: 'A herbaceous plant not valued for use or beauty, growing wild and rank, and regarded as cumbering the ground or hindering the growth of superior vegetation.' This definition is a useful starting point but it conceals more than it tells.

Flowers in the wild

Weeds are generally herbaceous plants – although they are at least as likely to be annual as perennial – and a few shrubs, like *Rhododendron ponticum*, are sometimes legitimately called 'woody weeds'. The dictionary is right in that they aren't, in the course of normal gardening, valued for their beauty or use, although some in truth are extremely attractive: think of the splendour of a mass of field poppies, a carpet of blue speedwell or a field of golden dandelions or meadow buttercups. These are all plants that would certainly be called weeds if they appeared among our vegetables, yet outside our gardens they are wild flowers. They do grow

wild and 'rank' or uncontrolled, even in gardens, in the sense that we haven't planted them; they may certainly 'cumber' or overwhelm the ground – think of chickweed or horsetail; and they very often hinder the growth of our 'superior' garden plants. But there's more to it than that, and here we come close to the true ethos of wildlife gardening.

Sharing our gardens

Conventional gardening – and, to be fair, that's what *The Oxford English Dictionary* is driving at – is humanitary or anthropocentric. We, as gardeners and garden owners, are all-important. Everything we do and grow in our gardens is based on our needs, and anything that operates counter to that is undesirable. Any plant that prevents our fruit, vegetables and flower borders from growing satisfactorily is an unwanted weed. Wildlife gardening is different. It's about sharing our gardens with other things, and sometimes growing plants that may be less attractive, less amenable to being cultivated, or of less direct use to us because they have some special merit for other creatures. Wildlife gardening is much less selfish and much more tolerant.

If you garden with any sort of wildlife consideration in mind, you will inevitably grow some plants that others will call weeds. Your flower borders may include some

Right The meadow buttercup (*Ranunculus acris*) would be treated as a weed if found growing in our cultivated gardens.

field poppies, they might even contain a clump of meadow buttercups. They are unlikely to include speedwell because it flowers for a very short time, and they are unlikely to include dandelions because they self-seed and spread so freely that before long your other plants will suffer. And never forget, the seeds won't stay in your own garden but will blow into those of your neighbours, too, and they might well be less enthusiastic about native plants than you are. Nonetheless, the more dedicated your garden or a part of your garden is to wildlife, the more so-called weeds you will have. But unless your wildlife garden is truly huge, you will never grow the really aggressive, competitive weeds like bindweed, ground elder, horsetail and creeping thistle because they are just too invasive and will very soon subjugate everything else.

In my garden, the borderline between what I will and won't accept is neatly exemplified by dandelions. These are very important for many insects in providing nectar relatively early in the season when little else is flowering – or at least flowering in such profusion. But their self-seeding means that they can easily swamp much else, so I don't grow them in my conventional garden where they would soon take over the lawn. I do, however, have them in the wildlife garden, but even here I compromise by using a long-handled weeding tool and pulling out at least half of the plants by hand every spring. It is a classic example of the fact that a dedicated wildlife garden isn't a care-free option. It needs management to succeed.

Native plants needing special care

Labelling a plant as a weed is nothing to do with where it originates. It's sometimes said that weeds are native plants reclaiming land that is rightfully theirs. But, in truth, most of our native plants are not and never could be weeds because they aren't vigorous enough, either in relation to each other or to some of the exotics grown in our gardens. This means that if we decide for whatever reason to grow them, they may actually need special care and attention to prevent them from being swamped.

Right The native common toadflax (*Linaria vulgaris*) is very beautiful and deserves a place in your wildlife garden, especially as it is the food of two particular moths: the toadflax pug (*Eupithecia linariata*) and the marbled clover (*Heliothis viriplaca*).

The native yellow-flowered common toadflax (*Linaria vulgaris*) is a case in point. I grow it in my wildlife garden partly because I think it very beautiful but also because it is the food plant of two interesting moths: the toadflax pug (*Eupithecia linariata*) and the marbled clover (*Heliothis viriplaca*). It is a poor competitor, however, and tends naturally to grow on waste ground, roadsides and among railway tracks, so I keep it in an area of relatively bare soil, free of other plants.

By contrast, some of the most aggressive and troublesome weeds are aliens that have been accidentally or deliberately introduced to this country where they now have free rein, away from their natural competitors and enemies that keep them in check in their place of origin. The top five most troublesome garden weeds today overall are probably Japanese knotweed, field bindweed, ground elder, horsetail and perhaps pink-flowered oxalis. Only two, field bindweed and horsetail, are British natives; the others were brought here as garden plants.

How people create pests

The notion that all insects are harmful and all animals that come into our gardens must be some form of pest is not quite as generally believed as the notion that all wild plants are weeds. But it is believed by some and, as this is a book about concern for wildlife in general, it's worth looking briefly at what turns a wild creature in some people's eyes into a pest.

Just like weed, pest is an artificial notion, and the dictionary definition again bears this out: 'Any animal, especially an insect, that attacks or infests crops, livestock, stored goods, etc.' Crops exist only because people grow them, so, in that sense, only people can produce pests. It is in relation to insects – and by implication, related small invertebrate creatures – however, that the term pest is most often used, as the dictionary definition indicates. And just as some of the most serious garden weeds are exotic plants that have been introduced here, generally artificially, so many of the most important garden pests are exotic species, too.

Bullfinches (*Pyrrhula pyrrhula*)

Bullfinches are excellent examples of a wild creature turned into a pest. In books on wild birds, they are grouped with other species of finch, like chaffinches, greenfinches and goldfinches, with no indication that they are significantly different. They are singled out, however, in books on garden pests because at certain times of the year they feed on the buds of fruit trees and bushes. If you don't have fruit in your garden, a bullfinch is just another species of bird. In this instance, one person's pest is another person's beautiful wild creature.

Greenhouse whiteflies from tropical America, woolly aphids from North America, soil-inhabiting eelworms from many warm parts of the world, along with scale insects, some species of ant, several species of woodlice and many others from mites to cockroaches are all alien introductions. In some instances they may have ousted native species but because they are so small and, until recently, relatively little studied, no one really knows.

Why wildlife garden?

Wildlife gardening shows a deep and genuine interest in wildlife itself. It can help to maintain the genetic diversity of home-grown plants, provide animals and insects with food that may be becoming increasingly scarce in the wild and, in a small way, compensate for loss of habitats – so protecting our declining species.

Many wildlife gardeners are enthusiastic and active bird watchers, many belong to conservation groups or local natural history societies and are country walkers and ramblers. Many, indeed, are naturalists first and gardeners second. If nothing else, I hope that the message of this book will bring people from both camps closer together.

Sometimes, however, I feel expectations are set too high, and it's only fair to say what gardening in a particular way can do for wildlife in the wider context, and what it can't. I have already hinted that wildlife gardening grew out of, and is part of, the global environmental concerns of the past half century, but can it really do much towards saving the planet?

Growing genuine native species

Let's look first at the growing of native plants in gardens. Common plants like meadow buttercup and field poppy may be less numerous than once they were, but self-evidently they are not under threat; they are certainly not going to die out in the wild. Growing them in your garden won't make any difference therefore to their overall status in the British flora. But what about rarer species? In the most recent survey of British plant life, over 1,750 native species were considered to be under some form of threat, and of them, around 350 were believed to be in some danger of extinction. This should, however, be put into its true context, as it doesn't mean in danger of total extinction from the planet. There are no plant species native to Britain that aren't also native to somewhere else – in other words, there are no true endemic species, although there are some sub-species and varieties that are unique to Britain. And, in truth, there are very few British plants that aren't more common somewhere else. That is not in any way to diminish the importance of our home-grown stock because, although the same species may occur in many different places, there will be features of its genetic make-up that are peculiar to each region and it is vital to maintain this genetic diversity. It's important therefore to retain genetically pure, genuinely British populations of these plants.

With a little planning, gardeners can help ensure that this genetic purity isn't eroded. If you grow plants that are native British species, it is essential to buy only those guaranteed by the nursery to be of genuine British origin. Otherwise, they will interbreed with the local population and, in so doing, introduce foreign genes. All good and reputable wild plant nurseries and seed suppliers now certify the origin of their plants as British, and you should patronise only those that do.

To summarise, I don't believe that growing native plants in your garden will, in a literal sense, help their global survival chances but it can help keep up the numbers of our native 'strains'.

Maintaining biodiversity

There is something else, however, about wildlife gardening that I do think is hugely beneficial, and it has less to do with plants than with animals. On the

Song thrushes (*Turdus philomelos*)

Snails are the favoured food of song thrushes but, as there are now fewer ditches at field margins and fewer places generally in farm fields where snails thrive and proliferate, the song thrush has had, as a result, insufficient food. Gardens have helped these birds significantly because they are generally replete with snails – and the more lettuces and other snail-prone plants you can grow, the more you are assisting the song thrush population.

one hand, by growing native plants, you may be providing all manner of creatures with a food that is becoming scarcer in the wild (I shall discuss elsewhere in the book just how much advantage they are likely to take of this). But more important still is that the garden will, in a small way, be providing compensation for the loss of habitats. I have long believed this to be the greatest contribution wildlife gardening can make to maintaining our biodiversity.

Modern farming, modern countryside management and modern life in general have denuded our country of many once common habitats. Some are easily recognised – the draining of wetlands, for example, means fewer places for aquatic birds and amphibians. And while one garden pond won't make much difference, many hundreds or thousands of garden ponds can, provided that enthusiasm doesn't replace reality. As places for frogs and newts to lay their spawn, 10,000 garden ponds will be almost as good as 16sq km of natural swamp, but don't get too excited because they will be no substitute whatever as breeding grounds for bitterns or reed warblers.

Other examples of habitat loss are less obvious and the compensations wildlife gardening can make are less apparent but at least as important. There's a good example of this among one of our most loved songbirds, the song thrush. Since the mid-1970s, song thrush populations have been on the decline but for a long while, no one seemed sure why. It became popular to point the finger of blame at magpies in the belief that they were, quite literally, killing them off. There was no evidence for this, however, and it is only relatively recently that research has revealed changes in agricultural practices to be largely at fault (*see above*).

To find out more about nature and conservation outside the garden, try the following organisations:

www.wildlifetrusts.org
www2.btcv.org.uk – British Trust for Conservation Volunteers
www.nhm.ac.uk – website of The Natural History Museum; type 'nature societies' in search for a list of local natural history groups

The decline in the countryside

It's hard to open a newspaper today without reading how cities are encroaching on the countryside, housing development is eating into open land and habitat after habitat is suffering. It is up to gardeners to do all they can, within reason, to help compensate as areas of 'natural' countryside continue to diminish.

Our consciences may be slightly salved when we read that significant numbers of new houses are to be built on 'brownfield' sites, conjuring up images of redundant railway yards and old factories rather than virgin water meadows, chalk hillsides and deciduous woods. The reality, however, is that huge numbers of houses are still being built on undeveloped greenfield land. A further blow to our national biodiversity was struck by two recent official reports. One report revealed that since 2000, the term 'brownfield' has been used to include former residential land and associated gardens. The other revealed that brownfield sites themselves are important habitats for many threatened species. Nonetheless, however you look at it, new housing development, new roads and changes in farming practices look likely to continue to diminish the area of 'natural' countryside for many years to come.

Sizing up Britain's gardens

I am almost as anxious in this book to dispel poorly founded notions about what impact gardeners can make as I am to promote environmentally friendly gardening. With that aim, I think it's worth putting the size of British gardens overall in a national context. No one has any truly accurate data but there seems to be a general reckoning that there are about 20 million gardens in Britain, with an average size of about 200 square metres, making a total of 4,000 square kilometres.

People tend to point out that this is roughly the same size as Somerset, implying that, collectively, gardens can be as good for biodiversity and wildlife as an entire English county. They can't, of course, mainly because gardens are little bits of land, separated by other bits of land that are very different in character.

While the habitat you create in your own garden might be ideal for a particular type of plant, a species of beetle or a wood mouse, you may adjoin a main road, a supermarket, bus depot or sewage works that will appeal to a very different range of creatures. Animals and plants that individually need more room than your garden in which to live won't be satisfied. I'll take two rather dramatic examples to illustrate my

Above Adjoining gardens with no distinct barriers between them allow small animals such as hedgehogs to roam freely.

Above Changes in farming practices have led to the disappearance of many meadows.

point. Among the most important animals in the countryside at large are big birds of prey, such as buzzards, and big mammals, like deer. There are a great many buzzards and a great many deer living in Somerset but almost none live in any of Britain's 20 million gardens – individually, the gardens just aren't big enough. No matter how they are managed, gardens will be of no help to a huge range of large, hungry, wandering creatures.

The value of adjoining plots

Nonetheless, something that is also commonly overlooked is the value and impact of housing estates, urban streets, villages and similar areas where gardens do juxtapose. A row of gardens with no significant barriers between them could be appealing to creatures

that do need larger areas in which to roam – perhaps not buzzards and deer but smaller creatures such as song birds and bats that need more space than a single garden and so have the opportunity to fly over several hundred metres of food-supporting habitat.

I haven't seen the observational data to prove it, but I would be surprised if the incidence of bats isn't greater over areas of adjoining garden than over small, isolated plots with unappealing areas around them. Nor have I ever seen an instance where like-minded neighbours have grouped together with a wildlife gardening purpose to blend and complement all their plots. It would be a most interesting exercise and a far more worthy endeavour than television makeover programmes that try to persuade all the neighbours in a street to paint their house fronts in the same style.

The garden oasis

I don't want to minimise the value of any garden, however, even a largely isolated one, and must draw attention to the value of what has become known as the garden oasis. As long as the garden isn't too isolated and it is no further from another food source than the normal daily flying distance of birds or insects, it can act as an oasis, providing food and water and shelter. And if there are other, comparable gardens some distance apart, they can collectively provide stopping places over considerable distances.

All this underlines the importance of gardeners working collectively, but how many gardening societies ever offer their members the opportunity of working together towards a common wildlife purpose? Perhaps my comments will stimulate some cooperative efforts and, if so, this automatically raises the question of just how large are the distances involved. How big is the daily flying range or the territory of a bird or an insect?

Much research on both subjects has been undertaken for all manner of purposes and it's not surprising that the distances and areas vary considerably. A pair of golden eagles, for example, will need an area of at least 30 sq km of wild, untamed highland gardens all to themselves and will not tolerate others of the same species nearby. By contrast, a pair of robins, another highly territorial species, needs half a hectare of garden plots to keep them satisfied. The lateral distances travelled by much less territorial creatures are similarly varied, and this has become of importance recently with concerns over the contamination of wild plants and crops with insect-transported pollen from genetically modified plants.

Honey bees, which are the most studied insects, will generally forage over a distance of about one kilometre from their hives. The distances that bats will travel from their roosts in a night vary enormously, even within species, from a few hundred metres to many kilometres but, like bees, they return to their starting point. A slightly different type of behaviour is seen in butterflies and moths. Some kinds stay close to where their caterpillar food plants grow and where they themselves were hatched. This seems especially true of those with common food plants that grow everywhere – there is no incentive for the adults to fly very far.

Above The larvae of the brimstone butterfly (*Gonepteryx rhamni*) feeds on buckthorn (*Rhamnus cathartica*), so planting it judiciously will lure them to your garden.
Far left A honey bee, shown here feeding on a field scabious, will forage at a distance of about one kilometre from its hive.
Left Robins are extremely territorial, and you will usually find only one pair per garden.

Building a butterfly breeding colony

If you have a large garden and appropriate food plants, there is the exciting prospect that you may be able to build up a more or less permanent breeding colony of your own with very little difficulty. That lovely spring butterfly, the orange tip, whose caterpillars feed on many very common members of the brassica family, such as garlic mustard (*Alliaria petiolata*), is a good example. There have been orange tips occurring naturally close to almost every garden I have owned and it hasn't taken long before I acquired my own colony.

Other species that feed on less common, more widely dispersed plants, with their larvae feeding on different plants from the preferred nectar flowers of the adult, may wander further. Gardens containing appropriate types of plant that are strategically positioned over longer distances may be especially advantageous in luring butterflies to new areas. The brimstone butterfly, another lovely spring species with its specialised larval food plants of buckthorn and alder buckthorn, is a good example of this. I hardly ever saw a brimstone in our village when I first moved here but judicious planting of buckthorn has lured them in and they now live and breed every year. If other gardeners in villages nearby did the same, a larger local population of brimstones should soon build up.

For more on the state of the countryside:

Conflicts in the Countryside: The New Battle for Britain, David Bellamy (Shaw & Sons, 2005)
www.naturalengland.org.uk – government agency for all aspects of the countryside and natural environment
www.scotland.gov.uk – website of The Scottish Executive, includes Environment and Rural Affairs Department

Attracting wildlife and encouraging breeding

It may be straightforward to attract insects or wild creatures to your garden by growing plants or putting out food you know will entice them, but how do you encourage them to stay and breed? The wildlife gardener can only provide the props, such as nesting boxes or hibernation sites, and let nature take its course.

Long before the current vogue for relatively sophisticated wildlife gardening, gardeners and the public at large appreciated the beauty of butterflies and wanted to attract more of them to their gardens.

Buddleja davidii attracts butterflies more successfully than any other garden plant (*see below*), although other plants do run it fairly close: I find Michaelmas daisies

Buddleja

It has been known since the end of the 19th century that one plant, the Chinese shrub *Buddleja davidii*, would attract butterflies better than anything, to the extent that it soon became known as the butterfly bush. I have seen nine different butterfly species on a large buddleja in my own garden at the same time, and I am sure other gardeners could better this. There is obviously something about buddleja nectar that is mesmerically appealing to a wide range of butterflies – and, indeed, to most insects because there are always plenty of bees, flies and other species on the blossom, too.

and the ice plants, related to *Sedum spectabile*, are next best, although in a recent survey, the top five after buddleja in terms of the number of butterfly species they attracted were lavender, aubrieta, hebe, scabious and red valerian (*Centranthus*).

There is absolutely nothing wrong with wanting to attract butterflies to feed in the garden because their beauty and overall appeal are undeniable. In exactly the same way, there is absolutely nothing wrong with having bird tables and other types of bird feeder to lure as many different species as possible (later in the book I shall suggest the best ways to do this). The only real difference in objective between attracting birds and attracting butterflies is that with birds we gain most of the pleasure from watching the feeding process, whereas with butterflies, it is simply their colourful presence that we enjoy.

Providing food for caterpillars

It was some time, however, before gardeners came to realise that buddlejas and other nectar-producing flowers do almost nothing to aid the long-term survival of butterfly species because they don't actively encourage them to breed. No butterflies lay their eggs on buddlejas, and whilst a surprising number of moth species do, it doesn't necessarily represent their most important food plant. I have always felt it was just this realisation that first stimulated the interest in what I can best call the modern approach to wildlife gardening that has evolved over the past 30 or so years.

Caterpillars and what they eat

Butterfly species	Principal caterpillar food plant
Small tortoiseshell *Aglais urticae*	Stinging nettle *Urtica dioica* **[above]**
Small white *Pieris rapae*	Brassicas
Large white *Pieris brassicae*	Brassicas
Red admiral *Vanessa atalanta*	Stinging nettle *Urtica dioica*
Peacock *Inachis io* **[above]**	Stinging nettle *Urtica dioica*
Green-veined white *Pieris napi*	Brassicas
Comma *Polygonia c-album*	Stinging nettle *Urtica dioica*
Painted lady *Cynthia cardui*	Thistles and stinging nettle *Urtica dioica*
Speckled wood *Pararge aegeria*	Cock's foot, couch and other grasses

I think it's fair to say that the biggest and most obvious difference between the planting in a traditional garden and a dedicated wildlife garden now lies in the number of plant species grown specifically to provide food for caterpillars. And the reason there is such a large difference between the two kinds of garden will be appreciated when the types of food plant needed by common garden butterflies are recognised. Taking the nine species of butterfly I found simultaneously on my buddleja as a representative sample, their caterpillar food plants are as detailed in the chart above.

With brassicas already providing food for three species of white butterfly, it took a considerable leap of wildlife faith for traditionally minded gardeners to plant stinging nettles, thistles and couch deliberately in their gardens. Clearly an area had to be set aside specially and the 'patch of stinging nettles' became the talismanic trademark of the committed wildlife gardener, although paradoxically a number of recent research studies have reached ambiguous conclusions about their value.

It's unarguable that stinging nettles are the food plant of some important, common and attractive butterflies but whether the insects really make use of them planted in a limited artificial manner is disputed. There are many plants, however, that do provide food for caterpillars in a garden context – and some that can be grown quite satisfactorily in a conventional garden, too. (See p.69 for more information on butterfly and moth food plants.)

Bird breeding sites

Significant numbers of people have been feeding garden birds and, to a lesser extent, providing nest boxes for them since the first quarter of the 20th century. For many years, however, both activities were pretty unsophisticated. The bird nesting box generally featured a small hole and was attractive to blue tits and great tits, but not much else. Bird feeding meant putting out kitchen scraps or peanuts – the latter, it now appears, were usually contaminated with aflatoxin. The fact that some bird species nest and breed in gardens naturally (that is, not in artificial nest boxes) was, of course, well known.

I would guess that most people today provide bird feeding sites in their gardens for the almost equally significant motives of enjoyment and to help the bird population survive. I would also guess that most people who place nesting boxes in their gardens still do so almost entirely for the pleasure of seeing young birds and their parents, giving little consideration to the impact they might might have on bird populations at large. This isn't surprising as it has only been within the past three or four years that detailed research has disclosed just how important gardens are as bird breeding sites. For many species, from collared doves to spotted flycatchers, gardens have been shown to be enormously significant. What the research hasn't yet revealed is the relationship between the incidences of bird nesting and bird feeding – if you put out food regularly, are birds more likely to use your trees, hedges and nest boxes for breeding?

Do what you can

Clearly, anyone engaging in active wildlife gardening, whether as part of their general gardening activities or in a specific and directed manner, will be helping different creatures in different ways. You can't do all things for all species but your garden can and should provide food, shelter and breeding and/or hibernation sites for at least some of them.

Above A bird table sited at the edge of a
flower bed provides plenty of opportunity
for a variety of birds to feed and also nest
or hide in the trees and shrubs behind.
Left Position a nest box somewhere secluded
in the garden and out of reach of predators,
such as cats.

Does organic mean wildlife-friendly?

In many people's minds, organic gardening and wildlife gardening are inseparable. Both are perceived as being underpinned by a wish to do as little harm as possible to the environment. But they aren't the same and it's important to appreciate just what organic gardening involves and the possibilities and limitations it offers.

Recycling waste

Making compost in your garden and recycling as much organic waste matter as possible should be a pivotal part of any good gardener's activities (*see p.204* for more information on recycling and composting). Many organic gardeners use redundant materials in all sorts of inventive ways. On allotment sites, for example, it's not unusual to see old CDs strung on wire or string as bird scarers, discarded carpets laid as pathways, or even old doors as cold frame covers.

I don't subscribe to the theory that pretty well all other waste should be recycled in the garden, however. Redundant fridges or old plastic storage sacks, for example, should be recycled at the local waste recycling centre. This is because every garden, whether or not it is organic and whether or not it has a committed wildlife purpose, should be aesthetically appealing; it should look as attractive as you can make it.

Organic gardening is as much about definitions as about sensible horticulture. And whilst there are several possible definitions, the one most people understand is that organic gardening means using plenty of compost, recycling as much material as possible, and only using chemical pesticides and fertilisers that have some natural plant or animal origin – or at best are simply dug from a hole in the ground and not made in a factory.

Organic or artificial fertilisers?

Some fertiliser use is essential in any garden, although dedicated wildlife gardens use less than most (*see p.36*). However, in deciding between artificial and organic kinds, whether they are 'natural' or factory-made is unimportant. This is because once the fertilisers are added to the soil, they begin to degrade into simpler chemical components. It is in this simple form that plants absorb them so by this stage, their origin is immaterial. Nitrogen to a plant is nitrogen whether it began life in ammonium sulphate or dried blood. On that criterion, therefore I can find no difference and I know of no evidence that inorganic (or 'artificial') fertilisers used correctly and in moderation, as all fertilisers should be, have any detrimental effect on garden wildlife or have any influence on the appeal of gardens to wildlife. But I do stress 'correctly' and 'moderation' – both bone meal and dried blood, left

Left An organic kitchen garden, complete with herbaceous plants.

accessible in small heaps on the soil surface, are extremely attractive to foxes and dogs! I am far more concerned with the practical issue of speed of action.

Overall, organic fertilisers like bone meal and dried blood degrade more slowly and therefore are effective over a longer period of time than their artificial equivalents. That is why I use them although the availability over recent seasons of excellent artificial slow-release granular fertilisers has rendered this attribute less significant.

Organic pesticides

Unlike fertilisers, pesticide usage in a modern garden needs some justification (as I explain on *p.196*). There are now relatively few products available and all gardeners are having to adjust to life without them. If a pesticide is considered necessary however, will an organic product be safer for garden wildlife?

My belief is emphatically not and the logic for imagining otherwise is one of the most irrational aspects of modern gardening. What conceivable basis can there be in believing that just because a substance originates

Below Derris, a pesticide used by organic gardeners, is toxic to ladybird beetles which prey on aphids.

in the natural environment, it is necessarily safe when processed and then returned to it, generally in relatively huge amounts?

Practically every organic pesticide has a broad-spectrum action; that is, it will kill a wide range of organisms, good and bad, quite indiscriminately. Derris, for example, the stand-by pesticide of many organic gardeners, is often said to be valuable because it is not harmful to beneficial insects like hover-flies and honey bees. It is, however, toxic to ladybird beetles and predatory mites, which means that it will diminish their numbers and so reduce their effectiveness as natural pest predators. It is also toxic to birds and acutely toxic to fish – it is used as a fish poison by native peoples in South America.

Another group of 'safe' pesticides that have become popular with organic gardeners are natural soaps and oils, including canola oil, which is obtained from rape seed. They appear to be harmless to humans but I have found it surprisingly difficult to track down any evidence of their effect on the environment at large and there's no doubt they are indiscriminate in their killing of insects – good, bad and indifferent.

Finally, I should say a word about what is perhaps the most contentious of the non-organic pesticides that remain available to gardeners and the product about which I am most often asked – slug pellets. Although there are organic chemical slug controls, I don't find them very impressive and no more effective than simple physical traps or barriers.

Slug pellets and liquid concentrates containing the chemical metaldehyde undoubtedly work. They kill slugs and snails but how harmful are they to other wildlife if the wildlife is allowed access to them? I can't give a definitive answer because the evidence I have seen is contradictory. One reputable authority, for example, says that metaldehyde is 'harmful to fish and other aquatic life'; another that 'available data suggest that metaldehyde is practically non-toxic to aquatic organisms'. Are the pellets harmful to creatures like hedgehogs and birds that pick them up and eat them? I don't know because I can't find any conclusive data; and in any event, the effects would depend entirely on the quantity eaten in a given period of time. Do I use them in my garden? No.

Non-toxic slug controls

Beer traps are effective and easy to make. Try cutting off the base of a plastic bottle, sinking it into the ground next to vulnerable plants, then filling it with beer [1]. Alternatively, cut the neck and shoulders from a plastic bottle. Invert this piece into the open end of the bottle, staple it into position to form the entrance to the trap, then add beer to the bottle and rest it on its side [2]. Another way to deter slugs is to cut a serrated collar from a plastic bottle with pinking shears [3].

cause scorching and other damage to a wide range of plants. Neither sulphur nor Bordeaux mixture are effective controls for more than a small proportion of the many kinds of microscopic fungi that cause plant diseases; and against bacteria and viruses, their action is extremely limited.

If you do have a serious plant disease problem and have no moral or ethical reason for not wanting to use a chemical spray, I see no reason why you should restrict your choice to a product with an organic label. Better it seems to use a synthetic fungicide, specifically created to do a particular task with the optimum reliability and minimal side-effects rather than some naturally occurring substance that just happens to have some fungicidal properties.

Use a pesticide or fungicide if you must therefore but look extremely carefully at the information on the label before making your choice. Full data must now be provided about activity and side-effects and it will repay you to read the small print. (For more information on specific pest and disease control without using chemicals, *see p.194.*)

Choosing a fungicide

There are very few fungicides still available for use in gardens and among them, sulphur, and a copper-based product called Bordeaux mixture are the only kinds with an organic label. Sulphur has low toxicity towards mammals and most other creatures although copper-based compounds do have mammalian toxicity and can

For more information on organic gardening, look at:

The Garden Organic, Allan Shepherd (Collins, 2007)
Organic Gardening, Geoff Hamilton (Dorling Kindersley, 2004)
www.gardenorganic.org.uk – website of the leading national charity for organic growing, includes lots of information on organic gardening techniques

Pests and diseases in the wildlife garden

Any description of conventional gardening invariably includes a consideration of pests and diseases. But no one seems to ask why they create problems for garden plants and not for those growing in the wild. Plants in the wild don't need pest and disease controls, so should the wildife gardener use them?

Let's be clear – pests and diseases weren't invented when people began to garden. They didn't materialise from thin air; and nor in most cases are they mutations of non-pest species. Every pest and every disease that creates a problem by feeding on plants in our gardens exists on a similar diet elsewhere. So why don't we notice them?

The first part of the answer is concerned with human nature. We don't own the plants in the fields and hedgerows. We didn't buy them, we don't pay for fertiliser to feed them and nor do we know them intimately through seeing them every day. They just don't matter as much to us and so we just don't notice if they are less than perfect. But look closely at the leaves of a meadow cranesbill (*Geranium pratense*) and

you may see geranium rust; look at the young shoots on the oak tree and you will very probably find oak mildew, and turn over the leaves of beech trees and you will very soon see colonies of the same aphid species that occurs on your garden hedge.

It's equally true that you rarely see wild plants devastated to the extent, for example, that garden nasturtiums or cauliflowers can be devastated by the caterpillars of the large white butterfly. That has to do with the nature of the nasturtium and the cauliflower and the way we grow them, and I'll try to explain this.

The balance of nature

One of the most freely used but rarely defined phrases in natural history is 'the balance of nature'. It means different things to different people but to me, it means the multitude of complex interactions and inter-relationships that exist between every living thing in a habitat and that result in the habitat appearing to us to be constant, unchanging.

If year by year, you look at an old hedgerow or a mature woodland, it seems to be more or less the same. The odd tree will fall, the odd clump of wild flowers spread a little but generally, what goes out is balanced by something else coming in. And this applies to the effects of pests and diseases. Imagine a large

Left Lady's smock (*Cardamine pratensis*) is eaten by caterpillars but plants in the wild soon renew themselves.

white butterfly arriving in a hedgerow, laying its eggs on the leaves of a wild brassica plant like garlic mustard (*Alliaria petiolata*) and then flying on to the next hedgerow where it may lay a few more, possibly on a related species like lady's smock (*Cardamine pratensis*). Perhaps living in or near the hedgerow will be a natural enemy of the caterpillars – an obvious one like a blue tit, which eats them whole, or something more insidious like an ichneumon wasp, which lays eggs on caterpillars so its larvae can parasitise them.

Some caterpillars will survive and some of the foliage of the hedge mustard and the lady's smock will be eaten or disfigured but aesthetically it doesn't matter. The damaged parts will soon be replaced by others that grow to take their place. The blue tit and the ichneumon wasp will move on to feed on other insects, just as the large white itself has moved on to lay eggs on a different host plant. No one living organism in the habitat has really

been adversely affected by the sequence of events; overall, the hedgerow looks the same – just a couple of tiny examples of what makes up the 'balance'.

But gardens aren't like that. Even the most stable parts of a garden – the shrubberies and perennial borders – change as we prune, take out, move around, re-arrange and re-stock. And some parts, the vegetable plot or annual flower bed most obviously, change beyond recognition from one season to the next.

There's not much balance of nature there. So let's look more closely at the nasturtiums and cauliflowers and discover specifically why they have been affected so badly and we shall see that almost everything that is different from the hedge can be laid at the hands of human actions.

The cauliflower is almost a native plant. Its ancestor, the wild cabbage (*Brassica oleracea*) certainly occurs on British sea cliffs, and it was one of the many cultivated forms – like Brussels sprouts, kohlrabi, broccoli and kale – to have been developed by breeders to be big and plump and tasty. But sometimes, when plants are bred in this way, other features, such as resistance to pests, may be lost. And breeding may not only remove resistance; it might enhance a character that a pest or disease finds appealing. The soft, fleshy tissues of the cauliflower may be more attractive to a caterpillar than those of the wild cabbage – just as they are to us.

The nasturtium raises another important matter. It originates from South America, where the large white butterfly doesn't occur. To put it simply, before 1684, no nasturtium had ever met a large white! So there had never been any opportunity for a population of nasturtiums to develop any resistance to large white caterpillars. Most of our garden plants are also exotics and in British gardens, they are encountering the local pests and diseases for the first time.

Garden monoculture

There's one other aspect of gardening that makes garden plants significantly different from wild ones and increases their likelihood of being seriously attacked by pests and diseases. In gardens, just as on farms, large numbers of individuals of one type of plant are often massed together. The most extreme examples are in annual flower beds and vegetable plots where row after row, or block after block, of one type of plant (very often one variety of one type of plant) are grown to the exclusion of everything else.

This is relatively unusual in the wild. Hedgerows, cliff-tops, banks of streams and woodland edges are all sites where there are, fairly obviously, mixtures of

Well-bred and exotic

Even before they were planted, the nasturtium and cauliflower had been interfered with. The nasturtium (*Tropaeolum majus*) isn't a native British plant. It is South American and wasn't introduced to European gardens until the end of the 17th century. And in the 300 years since, it has been crossed, selected and altered by plant breeders.

species. But so very often are natural woods and areas of natural grassland. We don't have many surviving natural woods in Britain and no natural grassland but examples exist that have been free of human interference for a long time and so provide acceptable replicas. If you look closely at these habitats, you will see that individuals or individual groups of one species tend to be dispersed among other species. This makes it more difficult for pests and diseases to travel between plants. A grass pest or a disease on one grass stalk, for example, can't hop directly onto the next grass stalk because there are unappetising sorrels, clovers and other plants in the way.

The significance of this in a garden is that a pest or disease arriving or landing on one plant in the row or bed has an easy passage onto others. For this reason, you should try to imitate nature in a conventional garden and have mixtures of plants in your beds and borders wherever possible.

In some circumstances, growing mixtures may be impractical – you might, for example, end up with vegetables growing to different sizes and at different rates. Nonetheless, the risks might make specialist growers of roses, chrysanthemums, dahlias and other 'hobby' plants think carefully about how they plant them. And in a dedicated wildlife garden, mimicking nature by having mixtures of many different species is hugely sensible.

Allowing nature to take its course

On balance, my belief is that you should do absolutely nothing directly to control pests and diseases in a dedicated wildlife garden, and certainly use no chemical control at any time. If one kind of plant does succumb, then accept it as a step in a self-selecting process by which the plants and animals that are best suited to your wildlife garden are those that will ultimately survive.

In a conventional garden managed with wildlife in mind, use the minimum of direct pest and disease control and then only if there is some serious threat to an important aspect of your gardening.

Human intervention

A very familiar garden disease reveals another side to the story. Groundsel (*Senecio vulgaris*) is an extremely common native British plant. It's a rather charming and fairly harmless annual weed that is worth tolerating in a wildlife garden because it provides food for a number of caterpillars.

Groundsel doesn't occur in Australia but related plant species there are affected by a rust disease fungus. The effects of the fungus on these plants aren't particularly devastating (because there's a balance of nature in Australia, too) and an equilibrium exists in which neither the fungus nor the native host plants are seriously threatened.

However, some imported *Cineraria* plants affected by the rust brought the disease from Australia to Britain, where it met groundsel, a plant with very conspicuously no resistance to it. Now it's almost impossible to find a population of groundsel in Britain that isn't affected by this disease - look in your own garden. And although groundsel is a wild plant, it doesn't negate my comment about wild plants not being devastated by diseases or pests because it was human intervention that bears the responsibility.

Using fertilisers

Why is it that wild plants obtain all the food they need whereas most garden plants require extra minerals in the form of fertilisers? The answer has nothing to do with the plants themselves but is about our own expectations and requirements as gardeners. So should fertilisers be used in the wildlife garden?

It's self-evident that no living thing will survive without food. On a number of occasions, however, I have been asked why garden plants need to be given artificial supplementary food in the shape of fertiliser. On the one hand, the question has arisen because of a misunderstanding about a process called photosynthesis, and on another because of a lack of appreciation of an essential difference between wild and garden plants.

Most gardeners know that photosynthesis is a process by which green plants manufacture their own food from carbon dioxide and water, using chlorophyll to trap the energy from sunlight and bring about the necessary chemical change. But plants cannot manufacture all their nutrient needs in this way and most importantly, they also require mineral substances which are absorbed through their roots from the soil.

When to fertilise

Plants in the wild obtain all the food they need because, unlike garden plants, they aren't required to live up to any human ideal. You only need to compare a wild carrot and a cultivated variety to understand what I mean. The wild plant is a pretty enough thing above ground but it has a thin, stringy root. While much of the difference between the wild carrot and its domestic descendant is the result of selective breeding, the extra feeding the garden plant receives also plays a significant part.

In a conventional garden, gardeners just wouldn't be satisfied with vegetables, flowers and fruit that were no improvement on their wild counterparts. Hence the need for fertilisers and, if you have a conventional garden that is simply being managed in a wildlife-friendly way, there's no reason to do anything differently from what you have always done.

The dedicated wildlife garden in large measure, however, is different. We want our native plants to look like native plants, and we want our wild flower meadow to be just that – a meadow of wild flowers – not a grassy lawn with a few sparse blooms surviving against the odds. Plants that thrive on large amounts of fertiliser – like grasses – will simply swamp everything else.

There are two significant exceptions to this general maxim. First, I always use bone meal when planting trees and shrubs, whether native or exotic. This is because it is important that they are properly established and encouraged to develop a good secure root system. Second, some fertiliser is also required in the miniature cornfield habitat for species such as corncockle, field poppy and corn marigold (*see p.164*).

Right Grasses thrive on fertiliser and would grow to the detriment of flowers if feed was applied to a wildflower meadow.

Why plants need nutrients

Among the major nutrients that plants need, nitrogen promotes the growth of leaves and shoots, magnesium is needed for chlorophyll production and phosphorus is important for the growth of roots.

Adapting your existing garden

To help you decide how much or how little time, effort and space you want to devote to the wildlife cause and how to balance an attractive and practical environment for your family against environmental motives, why not do a wildlife audit of your existing garden. It can be as brief or as detailed as you wish.

Most gardeners inherit the basis of their gardens from a previous owner of the property and it's a fact that a large number hardly ever change anything, either in terms of the plants or the overall design. The inconvenient twists and turns of the lawn that add to the work of mowing remain, along with the overgrown conifers that draw nutrients and moisture from the surrounding beds and borders.

So why not make a 'wildlife audit' of your existing garden? Simply look at each plant or group of plants and each structure or design feature in your garden and then, by using the information you will glean from this book, create a checklist from which you can weigh up their relative merits and your possible options.

In the chart on the following pages I have given an example of the type of appraisal I have in mind. It is in truth an interesting exercise and makes you really look at your garden, irrespective of the conclusions you draw from it. I do want to stress, however. that no-one should feel compelled to make any changes or feel guilty if they don't, although I happen to believe if you are reading this book, you have at least some wish to know and do more than you have previously.

Overleaf is an example of a possible wildlife audit in a small garden.

Top right A small garden pond makes an attractive feature in any garden and will appeal to insects and other small creatures.
Right An apple tree on the lawn provides a stunning display of blossom in spring and attracts both insects and nesting birds.

A possible wildlife audit in a small garden/1

Feature	Garden value	Wildlife value	Action
Small front lawn mown weekly and fed twice a year with fertiliser and weedkiller	High – attractive in return for little effort	Moderate – low	None
Medium-sized back lawn mown weekly and fed twice a year with fertiliser and weedkiller	Moderate – attractive but in return for fairly high maintenance	Moderate – low	Possibly convert part to a wildflower meadow or retain as lawn but use only fertiliser and not weedkiller
Small rock garden	Low – attractive in spring only	Low	Replace with bed of native flowers
Large holly tree on rear boundary	Moderate – provides screening and shelter	Moderate – fruits provide food for birds	Erect nesting box in the tree
Flowering cherry on front lawn	Low – good in spring but not much interest thereafter	Low	Consider replacing with tree providing blossom and ornamental fruits for birds
Tub of petunias and busy lizzies by front door	Moderate – but needs watering, feeding and deadheading	Low	Retain tub but choose better plants for pollen and nectar
Daffodils in bed by front lawn	Moderate – good in spring but nothing thereafter	Low	None – but perhaps consider having a mixture of smaller, neater bulbs to provide a longer flowering season
Small plum tree in kitchen garden [right]	Moderate – attractive blossom and then good fruit	Moderate – good for insects when in flower and fruit	None

Feature	Garden value	Wildlife value	Action
Large old apple tree on back lawn	Moderate – attractive blossom and then a few fruits	High – flowers and fruit good for insects and branches for nesting birds	Erect nesting box in the tree
Island bed in lawn	High – provides range of flowers in summer	Moderate – depending on species, provides pollen and nectar	Check flowering times of flowers and possibly replace some with others that give longer season and better nectar
Small frost-free greenhouse	High – provides space to store plants in winter, propagating area and a tomato crop in summer	Low – except indirectly in providing seedling plants for use in the garden	Consider raising some native plants from seed for planting out
Leyland cypress hedge round back garden	Moderate – not attractive but provides shelter and privacy	Low – provides some cover for nesting birds	Consider replacing a few plants with native hedging species
Herb bed **[left]**	High – attractive and useful	Moderate – good for insects when in flower	Retain and include wider range of herbs
Small vegetable patch	High – provides produce for kitchen	Moderate – insects and birds feed on produce	Possibly provide protection for some crops
Plastic compost tumbler	Moderate – produces valuable compost but in small quantities	Low – nothing can gain access although compost provides useful habitat once placed on soil	Consider replacing with open compost bin
Small ornamental pond with small fountain and goldfish	High – pleasing to look at and listen to in return for minimal effort	Moderate – will attract some insects and other small creatures which will lay eggs and breed	None
Small wooden shed	High – storage of garden goods	Low – provides shelter for hibernating insects	Possibly add trellis with a climber and hibernation boxes to the outside.

Starting from scratch

If you are one of thousands of gardeners who move to a new house with a virgin plot, you have lots of available options. Before making a list of the wildlife features you might consider, try to appraise the garden and your future gardening activities as a whole, in particular the amount of time you will have to devote to them.

Ask yourself if you want solely an ornamental garden or if you expect your plot to feed you. Do you hope to grow vegetables, and if so, do you want to grow them to the level of being self-sufficient? Do you plan to have fruit and if so, which are your priorities – soft fruit, tree fruit or both? But none of these questions can be considered in isolation from the equally essential matter of the time you have available. Over the years my objective has always been the same – I want to make gardening as enjoyable as it can be for as many people as possible. I assume no-one really wants to spend most of their time weeding, watering, feeding or repairing paths.

But what about the time available overall? Like most people, will you only be able to spend time in the garden at weekends? Are you away from home during the week and unable even to attend to essential watering at the height of summer? Or does your work take you right away from home, out of the country perhaps, for weeks on end? And of course, the present trends in our climate and the water restrictions that seem destined to become part of our gardening future may mean that depending on where you live, watering to any significant extent may just not be a option.

Choosing lower-maintenance plants

Only you can answer these questions but I can at least suggest aspects of gardening that might prove difficult in various situations. Plants most in need of constant care and attention are fast-growing annual bedding plants and vegetables that have highly productive lives to pass through in the space of a few months.

With shallow roots they will need food and water for much of the summer. Despite the obvious courses of optimising the use of such water as is available – with rain butts, other water storage options and recycling,

Left Raspberries are relatively easy to grow so are ideal for people who have a limited amount of time to spend in the garden.

the extensive use of annual bedding plants is likely to prove a disappointment. And unless vegetables have a fairly regular water supply through the summer, a large vegetable garden is an unrealistic proposition. Fruit offers a much simpler, less demanding and rewarding means of supplying at least some of your culinary needs and even gardeners who spend a good deal of time away from home do grow excellent soft fruit.

I can only add that my dedicated wildlife garden with its native plants, although not an easy-care option, is at least one area of my garden that never, ever needs additional watering. I would like to think this might make wildlife and native plant gardening increasingly appealing to drought-stricken gardeners.

The elderly and children

There are other considerations before you begin to map out your garden and start. Elderly or infirm gardeners scarcely need to be reminded that it is the jobs necessitating bending that cause the greatest discomfort. A lawn and a few raised beds can make the difference between a garden being a worrisome chore and a joy.

Children in a garden can be a mixed blessing. It can be hugely rewarding to introduce them to the joys of gardening; after all, they are the gardeners of the next generation and the biggest mistake any parent can make is to exclude them from gardening even if they must be steered away from parts of it. And whilst the very young have an almost compelling urge to uproot whatever you may plant, there is no better antidote than to provide them with their own small area and their own few plants – but somewhere with sunshine and good soil; not please a miserable corner in which you can't produce anything yourself.

And, once again, pressing my wildlife gardening cause, I can only add that every year I entertain a small group of seven and eight year old children with an outdoor lesson in my own garden, and the wildlife area is the part to which they are drawn to like a magnet. The mix of natural history and horticulture is something they clearly find as compelling as I do.

Above Children of all ages enjoy gardening especially if given their own small area to look after, with a few plants, miniature tools and a watering can.

Children and water

One golden rule must be that small children and garden pools do not mix. If you plan to build a pool, delay it until they are old enough to appreciate the dangers of water or alternatively follow my practice and ensure that it is an area, such as a discrete dedicated wildlife plot, that can properly be fenced and access to it can be secure.

ATTRACTING WILDLIFE

In this part of the book, I look at how to encourage birds, mammals, amphibians and reptiles, insects and other inverterbrates into the garden and create the kind of conditions that might tempt them to stay and breed. I end by describing the types of plants that should be encouraged to grow in the garden because they need to be preserved. These plants, which include mosses and ferns, together with fungi, also provide essential food and habitats for all kinds of creatures.

You can't and won't attract all animals, even everything that appeals to you, because there must already be a natural population not far away. For example, no matter what you do, red squirrels are unlikely to come into your garden unless you live in one of the few areas of Britain - such as the English Lake District, parts of East Anglia, Scotland or the Isle of Wight - where they live naturally.

And although birds are more mobile and travel further distances than mammals, many of them, too, are restricted to certain parts of the country and/or to areas with particular habitat types. You won't, for example, see moorhens far from water, or Dartford warblers outside the south and east of England.

Making a difference

If you lower your sights and keep your expectations in line with reality and common sense, you can achieve a huge amount. Although we have a reasonably large bird population in the vicinity of our village, I am always amazed at the difference a little effort can make. The numbers of birds in our garden increased appreciably when 10 years ago I began my dedicated wildlife area. Time and again, I see evidence that putting out food for them is remarkably effective in enhancing their numbers.

If we are away for more than a week or so, and the bird feeders aren't topped up, I find the numbers of birds to be seen and heard on our return has declined dramatically. Sometimes, it can take another week or more to restore the situation. And bird feeding is so valuable for people with small plots who simply don't have space to set aside whole areas for wildlife. Of course, the discovery that putting out food will attract birds isn't exactly rocket science but I hope I can show the importance of doing it with some planning and thought and by using the appropriate food for each species.

Below left Red squirrels may visit your garden if you live in one of the few areas of Britain where they still thrive.
Below right Moorhens are never far from water, so you may see them if you live near to a river or lake.

Relatively few kinds of birds are generally perceived as unwelcome in gardens – magpies, feral pigeons, gulls and herons possibly, jackdaws and crows perhaps although there is little we can do to keep them away. Deterrent and scaring devices are available but some will scare away desirable species, too. It's important to remember that legally, scaring devices must not be used close to the nest of a Schedule 1 bird species (*see box, below*). Nor should any scaring device be placed so that it prevents nesting birds access to their nest; and nor of course should it cause any injury or harm.

Birds of prey, such as sparrowhawks, might not be universally welcomed in gardens because they attack smaller and more endearing species but again, there isn't much that can be done to persuade them to hunt elsewhere; and in any event, it's most important to realise that you can't and shouldn't try to 'cherry pick' your wildlife. Sparrowhawks catch sparrows and other small birds; that's the way it is and sometimes they will do it in your garden.

When we consider mammals, the situation is rather different. While we want to be able to lure hedgehogs and bats to our gardens, most gardeners would rather not actively encourage mice, voles, foxes, rabbits, or deer because of the damage they can do. Plants are different again. Apart from those we consider weeds, there really aren't many native flowering plants that are likely to arrive of their own volition and in truth there is little we can do to encourage them; although occasionally, a chance and interesting seedling will turn up.

Below Moss will easily colonise old roofs and walls.

None of this matters much because, unlike animals, we can simply introduce the plant species we want by sowing or planting them. Much more important and much more ignored are fungi and lower plants (mosses, liverworts and ferns). All are difficult, if not impossible, to plant but we can do a huge amount to provide conditions in which they will establish naturally.

Legal protection of birds and other creatures

Birds and other wild creatures are protected principally by the Wildlife and Countryside Act 1981, which has been amended several times. Under this legislation, birds and other creatures are placed in categories depending on their rarity and vulnerability. A Schedule 1 bird species is one that is protected by special penalties, either during a 'close season' or, for certain species, at all times. There are around 80 of these specially protected birds, with barn owls, tree creepers, redwings and fieldfares among those species likely to occur in gardens.

Birds

No area of wildlife interest can have seen such a meteoric rise as that relating to birds. In 1960, membership of the Royal Society for the Protection of Birds (RSPB), was only 10,000; today it is over 1 million. The range of bird feeds, feeders and nest boxes has increased correspondingly, giving wildlife gardeners plenty of choice.

To attract birds to the garden, I can't stress too highly the value and importance of providing natural foods in the shape of fruiting trees and shrubs and seeding perennials as well as regularly cultivating soil to turn up appealing insect larvae and other invertebrates. But many gardens are too small to be able to provide more than a token gesture towards the local birds' needs and in all gardens, the natural should be supplemented by the artificial.

It's within the memory of many gardeners today that 40 or 50 years ago, while a number of gardens had a bird box and a bird table, and sometimes a bird bath too, the devices were unsophisticated. The bird box was a simple, often homemade device with a single small hole and the bird table was also likely to be a DIY construction.

Today, things have changed beyond measure – at the last count, I found a leading manufacturer offering over 50 different kinds of bird feeder and numerous types of

Above Peanuts are best placed in mesh feeders within squirrel-proof cages.
Left Black sunflower seeds, which are high in nutritious oil, in a transparent tubular bird feeder.
Far left An adult blackbird with its nest of chicks is not too rare a sight, as blackbirds are common in suburban gardens.

nest box. No one is likely to want them all in their garden so it's worth examining which really work.

The value of putting out food to attract birds is fairly obvious but for many years that, too, was unsophisticated – kitchen scraps, peanuts, bread – much of it of little nutritional value and some of it potentially harmful. Today, careful research has resulted in a wide range of foods being sold, some supposedly tailored for certain kinds of bird. Blackcap mixtures, for example, contain dried insects as well as peanut flour although how effective they are in specifically attracting blackcaps isn't obvious. But whereas 30 or 40 years ago, make-do bird foods attracted perhaps 10 or so different species, many more can now be expected. As an indication of what the lucky gardener might anticipate, in 2002 a red kite became the 162nd species to be seen at volunteers' garden feeding stations in the British Trust for Ornithology Garden Bird Feeding Survey.

Planning bird feeding

If you do wish to lure a wide range of birds to your garden – and, more importantly, significantly help their overall survival, your bird-feeding activities need to be planned. First, you should take account of the way the birds feed naturally and which artificial feeding method they will prefer. Are they more likely to eat food on the ground or on a bird table? Will they hang from tubular feeders (both transparent seed tubes with feeding holes or 'ports' and mesh peanut containers), or peck at lumps of more or less solid food?

In my own garden of about one acre, I have three bird tables, two peanut feeders, eight tubular seed feeders and one cake formulation. I find I can just about keep pace with the rate at which these are depleted. Bird tables may be fixed on posts or hung from branches or other supports but they should always have some form of cover to keep the food dry. Tubular feeders are available in various lengths – the largest I have seen was 120cm long. It had 12 feeding holes and held 3.5kg of food.

The longer the feeder and the greater the volume of available food, the larger the number of birds; and so while the required frequency of filling doesn't alter, the cost of buying the food does. There's no point having more feeders or larger feeders than you have the time and money to service – bear in mind the industry statistic that 80 per cent of garden bird feeders are thought to be empty at any one time!

Tubular feeders may be hung from bird tables, special support posts (which are useful in tiny courtyard gardens) or from branches. Purpose-made inexpensive hooks of various lengths are available and are invaluable for hanging feeders in trees.

All feeders should be cleaned regularly – a 'bottle brush' will be needed for tubular feeders – to prevent the build up of diseases in old food that may affect birds or occasionally, even people. Environmentally friendly cleaning chemicals are available.

Next, give some thought to where the feeders should be positioned. In general, they are probably better in the open so the birds are aware of any predators approaching. Although it is sometimes said that feeders shouldn't be close to bushes from where cats may ambush the birds, I have never found this a problem. On the contrary, I find that having a bush nearby gives the birds security. It also helps to have a perch of some kind close at hand where the birds can wait to see if the coast is clear.

Feeders should be placed somewhere fairly quiet – certainly not at a roadside – but a balance needs to be struck because if they are a long way from the house, you will be denied the pleasure of seeing them. It's important to move bird feeders around the garden from time to time to prevent contaminating debris building up in the same place.

Right Tits are agile feeders and love pecking on peanuts.

Common garden birds and their favoured foods

Bird species	Favoured food
Blackbird	Live food, peanut granules, fruit
Blackcap	Peanut granules, fruit, live food
Blue tit	Peanuts, cake mixes, sunflower seeds, seed mixes
Brambling	Small seed in mixes, live food
Bullfinch	Sunflower seeds, seed mixes
Chaffinch	Peanut granules, seed mixes
Coal tit	Peanuts, cake mixes, seed mixes, sunflower seeds
Collared dove	Seed mixes
Dunnock	Peanut granules, small seeds in mixes
Goldfinch	Seed mixes, sunflower seeds, peanuts
Great spotted woodpecker	Live food, peanuts, cake mixes, sunflower seeds, seed mixes
Great tit	Peanuts, cake mixes, seed mixes, sunflower seeds
Green woodpecker	Live food
Greenfinch	Sunflower seeds, seed mixes
House sparrow	Sunflower seeds, seed mixes, live food
Long-tailed tit	Peanuts, peanut granules, cake mixes, sunflowers seeds
Nuthatch	Sunflowers seeds, peanuts, cake mixes
Pied wagtail	Live food
Robin	Live food, peanut granules
Siskin	Sunflower seeds, peanuts, small seeds in mixes
Song thrush	Peanut granules, fruit, live food
Starling	Almost anything
Wood pigeon	Seed mixes
Wren	Live food, peanut granules

Types of food

It really isn't practical to try and cater for each and every species with a purpose-made mixture and after many years of experimentation, I have come down in favour of the following five foods:

Black sunflower seeds [1] These are high in nutritious oil and can be bought in the husks or, at about twice the price, already shelled. The shelled seeds or kernels, usually called sunflower hearts, are probably worthwhile in small, neat gardens because the husks can be unsightly as the birds drop them (although they do make an excellent mulch in large containers, *see p.52*). When the husks fall to the ground, they also offer an incentive for ground-feeding species, like thrushes, blackbirds and chaffinches, to come and explore them. If you provide both shelled and unshelled seeds, you will probably find the birds ignore the latter. I place sunflower seeds in transparent tubular feeders although some are also included in the mixed feed (*below*).

Peanuts [2] It's especially important to buy these from a reputable source as inferior quality or incorrectly stored peanuts may be contaminated with a toxic mould. Never use salted nuts. I always put peanuts into mesh feeders with squirrel-proof cages. Although I have tried so-called decoy feeders – peanuts in boxes that squirrels can open – I find the theory that they will then leave bird feeders alone to be unproven.

Proprietary cake formulations [3] These are usually based on tallow but with additions designed to appeal to specific types of bird – tallow and peanut flour for example to attract tits, greenfinches, chaffinches, woodpeckers and nuthatches. These are hung from the bird tables.

Live food [4] While it isn't practical to supply it all the time, I do place live food in dishes on the bird tables once a week during spring when young birds are being fed and occasionally throughout the rest of the year. Live food could be earthworms, red worms from the compost bin, other larvae unearthed in the garden or purchased mealworms or waxworms. Although appreciated by many different birds, live foods have the advantage of attracting almost exclusively

Above A chaffinch pecks at mixed seeds on a bird table.
Left Different types of food will attract a more diverse range of birds.

insectivorous species, such as wrens, which otherwise seldom appear at feeders.

Mixed feed [5] I recommend using a mix containing a range of different ingredients and putting some in tubular feeders and some on bird tables. This is very important as it attracts such a range of species and if you are only supplying one kind of bird food, this should be it. By and large, you will get what you pay for. A cheap mixture may contain oatmeal, kibbled maize and cereals and will be appreciated by many birds. A more expensive blend to appeal to a considerably greater number of species might include black sunflower seeds, sunflower hearts, peanut granules, kibbled maize, millet, nyjer seed, rapeseed, safflower seed, pinhead oatmeal, canary seed and hemp. Other ingredients like naked rolled oats, raisins, sultanas, peanut granules, mixed corn and flaked maize are often used in mixes intended for ground-feeding birds such as dunnocks, thrushes and robins. You can, of course, buy all the basic ingredients and mix your own but will need to have somewhere dry and rodent-proof to store them all. Clear plastic containers with airtight clip-on lids are ideal. Never store any bird food (especially peanuts) in paper or cardboard containers in sheds or garages because rodents will find them just as soon as your back is turned.

Timing bird feeding

The timing of feeding was once thought much more significant than it is now and the general advice was not to supply food (apart perhaps from live food) when young birds were in the nests, the view being that it could be harmful.

Now the advice is to feed all year round but to avoid putting out whole peanuts in the nesting season because these could choke young birds. As I only ever put peanuts in mesh containers where they must be pecked into small pieces, I don't really change my feeding practices at all during the course of the year.

It's also most important to provide clean water. The simplest way to do this is with a garden pond or other water feature in which the fountain is kept running all year round so it never freezes over. I don't want to insult anyone's intelligence but I feel duty bound to report that it has been known for people to add anti-freeze to bird water in the belief that this will help! If a 'bird bath' is used, the water must be changed regularly.

Nesting sites

Just as with bird feeding, it's important to appreciate that different birds have different requirements for nesting sites. Curiously, it is only very recently that the real benefits of gardens in aiding bird breeding have been demonstrated and for some species, the importance of the garden habitat is truly huge.

Apart from ground-nesting species, which are rather unlikely to find a sufficiently undisturbed spot in gardens, most other habitats can be catered for – trees, shrubs, hedges, holes in walls and other places, and under the eaves of buildings. Larger gardens might even attract species that nest in holes in big old trees. (For more information about the choice of trees, shrubs and hedges for wildlife see *Managing different habitats, pp.80–143.*)

Of course, not all gardens can offer a full range of natural habitats and it is here that artificial nest boxes come into their own. It is important to appreciate

Above Small, open-fronted nest boxes are preferred by several birds, including robins, pied wagtails and wrens.

however that invaluable as nest boxes are, they cannot be a complete substitute for natural sites because some species will never use them. As I have mentioned, basic bird boxes have been placed in gardens for many years but today the range is huge and every serious wildlife gardener needs several. Not every box will be used, and certainly not every year, so you need have no fear about erecting too many. I have about 12 boxes in my own garden and I would estimate that perhaps one third are used at any one time.

Birds are fussy about where they will nest and I have placed what seem to me to be perfect nest boxes in ideal places only to find birds nesting nearby in some

Types of nest box required by birds that use them

Nest box	Bird species
Small hole – 25mm [1]	Blue tit, coal tit, great tit
Small hole – 32mm	Grey wagtail, house sparrow, nuthatch, pied flycatcher, tree sparrow
Medium hole – 45mm	Green woodpecker, lesser spotted woodpecker, starling
Large hole – 70mm	Little owl
Large hole– 150mm	Jackdaw
Large hole 200mm	Tawny owl
Small open front [2]	Pied wagtail, robin, spotted flycatcher, wren
Large open front	Kestrel
Special – open cup	Swallow
Special – closed cup with hole	Swift, house martin
Special – platform	Blackbird
Special – small triangular hole	Treecreeper

more natural or already existing spot. My old disused well-head pump, for example, is used every year without fail by great tits while they hardly ever use a nest box.

Nest boxes to cater for most of the garden bird species that will use them fall into about 10 types – small hole entrance, medium hole entrance, large hole entrance, small open front, large open front, platform and open cup with the addition of two or three specials (*see box, above*).

It's perfectly possible for DIY enthusiasts to make their own – even the cup-shaped boxes for house martins and swallows can be moulded from papier-mâché – but excellent proprietary boxes made from wood, resin, concrete and other materials are now available. Some are really rather beautifully made with thatched roofs – although their durability varies.

For more information about birds in your garden and how to attract them, check out the following:

Gem Garden Birds, Stephen Moss (Collins, 2004)
Garden Bird Songs and Calls, Geoff Sample (Collins, 2001)
www.rspb.org.uk – Royal Society for the Protection of Birds
www.birdfood.co.uk, *www.wigglywigglers.co.uk*, *www.wildforms.co.uk* – suppliers of nest boxes, feeders and much more besides

Mammals

Most gardens have a more or less resident population of at least a few native mammals – generally wood mice *(Apodemus sylvaticus)* and either bank voles *(Clethrionomys glareolus)* or field voles *(Microtus agrestis)*. Here's how to encourage more visitors, and manage those that could cause problems in the garden.

In addition to wood mice and voles, other mammals that are likely to visit gardens are shrews, dormice, moles, brown rats, grey squirrels, rabbits and hedgehogs. Bats may visit, too, but because they are nocturnal we don't often see them.

In large gardens, you might also spot weasels, stoats, badgers, deer and foxes. While all these animals may be fascinating to see at close range, some are likely to cause damage in a garden and their presence may need managing.

Above The dormouse is a rarely seen nocturnal animal found in deciduous woodland and overgrown hedgerows.
Right Hedgehogs travel between 1–2km each night in search of food.

Shrews, dormice, weasels and stoats

The common shrew *(Sorex araneus)* is especially common in gardens. Its natural habitat is among dense grass and other vegetation in woods and at woodland edges, often burrowing below ground and feeding on earthworms, beetles, spiders, slugs, snails and other invertebrates. Areas of rough grass in gardens – and wildlife gardens in particular – will always attract them. Dormice *(Muscardinus avellanarius)* are fairly rare and local in their distribution, although they may come into gardens close to woodland. The Mammal Society *(see box, p.63)* suggests erecting bird boxes with the hole facing a tree trunk specifically to attract them. Weasels *(Mustela nivalis)* and stoats *(Mustela erminea)* are important predators of rodents and rabbits but are intolerant of the presence of humans and are likely to become established only in larger, fairly wild gardens.

Hedgehogs

Primarily nocturnal, hedgehogs may benefit the gardener by reducing the slug and snail population. Those who are in doubt about the presence of hedgehogs in their garden at night will be convinced by the tell-tale elongated black droppings on the lawn. Hedgehogs will travel considerable distances in the course of a night to find food, and a garden with a population of slugs and snails will always be appealing to them. Artificial food is generally taken by hedgehogs when it is provided and may also help to attract them.

Cats and wildlife

· ·

The most common mammals in most gardens are cats; and therein lies a problem. There are about 1 million feral cats – domestic cats gone wild - in Britain, which aren't very important in a wildlife context. By contrast, a recent survey by the Mammal Society revealed that the domestic cat population - cats owned as family pets - comprises the main predators of British wildlife, and most especially in gardens.

The survey estimated that 57 million mammals, 27 million birds, 5 million reptiles and amphibians and 3 million other creatures were killed by cats annually. This need come as no great surprise when it is realised that the garden-inhabiting domestic cat population of around 9 million animals is six times greater than that of all wild terrestrial predators combined!

The message is pretty straightforward: if you want to attract wild creatures to visit or live in your garden, owning a cat won't help.

It goes without saying that hedgehogs must be able to gain access to your garden and there is no easy answer to providing a boundary that will admit them but exclude rabbits, cats and other less desirable intruders. It's important to bear in mind that although technically they are insectivores, this shouldn't be interpreted to mean hedgehogs only eat insects – in fact, they are moderately omnivorous. They should not, however, be given bread and milk because there is evidence this can cause diarrhoea and other afflictions. It may also harm the animals' teeth. Proprietary hedgehog food contains dried insects, meat, nuts, fruits, honey and other suitable ingredients although when providing dry food of this type, a dish of clean water should also be supplied.

There is no need to provide special shelter for hedgehogs although hedgerows, shrubberies, compost heaps and gaps beneath sheds or other garden buildings will be appreciated. Proprietary wooden hedgehog boxes are also available or could easily be made from untreated timber. A small entrance 'tunnel' will help deter predators (like badgers or dogs) from gaining access.

Compost heaps and leafmould cages are especially welcome because they provide good hibernation sites – but be very careful when lighting bonfires because hedgehogs often hide among the piles of prepared debris. For several years, a hedgehog hibernated in a pile of leaves that accumulated at the base of an old wisteria growing against the wall of our house – all that was needed on my part was not to be too scrupulous in tidying the garden in the autumn. It may have been the same animal each time although hedgehogs are not thought to live much longer than three years in the wild. The British Hedgehog Protection Society (*see p.63*) gives advice on the care and conservation of hedgehogs.

Bats

· · · · · · · · · · · · · · · · · · · ·

The objective of attracting bats lies in the pleasure of watching them in the evening and of knowing that we are helping animals that nationally are under serious

Above The brown long-eared bat (*Plecotus auritus*) is the second most common garden bat.

threat. But it's a bizarre paradox that these are the mammal species most people spend most time in protecting yet are creatures they have never seen at close quarters, would tend to shy away from if given the opportunity, and which are all but impossible to identify by the lay observer when on the wing.

There are probably 17 native types of bat (there is uncertainty about one or two which may or may not still occur in Britain) but 90 per cent of the British bat population belongs to one species, the tiny common pipistrelle (*Pipistrellus pipistrellus*). Overall, probably the second commonest garden bat is the spectacular brown long-eared bat (*Plecotus auritus*) but the likelihood of seeing other kinds of bat depends on the part of the country in which you live (there are more species in southern England than elsewhere in the British Isles) and the types of vegetation and habitat that occur locally. Daubenton's bat (*Myotis daubentonii*)

for example, favours rivers and lakes, Natterer's bat (*Myotis natteri*) open farmland, and the splendid noctule (*Nyctalus noctula*), parks and woodland. Most bats feed on insects and most species catch them in flight. There is little that can be done to lure them into gardens by providing food therefore, although the presence of a garden pond and plenty of flowers, both of which attract insects, will indirectly prove beneficial.

It probably also helps to provide artificial roosting boxes, popularly called bat boxes. I say 'probably' because although large numbers are sold, many gardeners (me included) have them in their gardens and conservation bodies like the various County Naturalists Trusts, local bat groups and the Bat Conservation Trust (*see box, p.63*) encourage their use, no one has been able to point out any data to me to prove how effective they are. It isn't known how many gardens have them and if the occurrence of bats has risen in consequence.

My advice is to use bat boxes in your garden; they may well prove effective although their potential is limited to the summer months. Bats, along with

Above Bat boxes should be placed as high as possible with plenty of space in front to make it easy for bats to fly in and out.

or three boxes is ideal. Remember that bats have special legal protection and may not be disturbed in any way. You can look for droppings underneath the box as an indication of occupancy but if bats are present, only someone with a special licence may examine it. If you do find that bats are using your box, notify your local bat group so that the information may be recorded.

Local experts will help you to identify bats although it is also possible to buy small 'detectors' that convert bats' ultra-sonic signals into audible sounds. If you stand in your garden in the evening, the equipment will certainly indicate whether bats are active and then by comparison with standard recordings, it is theoretically possible to identify species – but it isn't easy!

Managing other mammals

Unfortunately, there are some visitors to the garden that may not be so welcome because of the damage they do to garden plants or the nuisance they cause. Among these animals are rabbits, grey squirrels, foxes, moles, mice, badgers and deer.

Rabbits will eat almost any garden plant, including grasses, root vegetables and young trees, as well as dig holes in hedgerows and elsewhere. Protect plants with chicken wire which should be turned outwards for 30cm at the base over the soil surface and pegged down. You can protect individual young trees with tree protectors.

Grey squirrels are attracted to gardens where food is available, particularly when there are easy pickings such as peanuts on bird tables. So if you feed garden birds, use squirrel-proof feeders (*see p.51*). Squirrels also have a habit of stripping bark from young trees, feeding on fruit crops, and uprooting and eating bulbous plants. Cover newly planted bulbs and peas and beans with 1cm-mesh chicken wire.

While some people like to feed foxes in the garden because they are enjoyable to watch, to others these animals create a real nuisance by uprooting plants, digging holes to bury prey, and raiding dustbins and compost bins. They can also make a great deal of noise, especially during the mating season. To help deter

dormice and hedgehogs, are the only British mammals to hibernate – for the very good reason that there isn't enough food available in the winter. Yet even for fairly well-studied bat species, the location of the hibernation sites is often unknown – it generally seems to be in underground holes, caves, beneath bridges, in hollow trees and similar places. What garden bat boxes do is provide temporary summer roosting places and possibly nursery roosts where young will be raised.

There are several patterns of proprietary bat box made from resin or rough timber (the roughness gives bats a better grip) and they are fairly simple to make from untreated timber. Positioning of bat boxes is as important as their design. They should be placed as high as possible, out of reach of cats, with plenty of free air space in front of them so bats can easily fly in and out. There is some evidence that boxes facing in different directions may be used by bats at different times of the season or in different weather conditions, so having two

Above Badgers usually visit gardens at night, when they may eat various plants and damage lawns, hedges and fences.

foxes, make sure that bins are fully secured so that they cannot forage for food. You may find that approved deterrent chemicals are partially effective, particularly if applied where droppings are regularly found.

Although moles can be beneficial in the garden by eating harmful insect larvae such as cock chafers and carrot fly, they are often regarded as pests because their burrowing creates mole hills of ejected soil that disfigure lawns and other areas. To discourage moles, special electronic ultrasound-emitting deterrent devices can be inserted in the soil.

Badgers are primarily nocturnal animals that are rarely seen during the day. If they enter the garden, they may uproot bulbs and tuberous plants, damage lawns by digging, eat fruit and vegetables and damage fences and hedges. They are protected under the Protection of Badgers Act 1992 (*see box, right*) and must not be harmed. To keep them out of the garden, the best option is to use low-voltage electric fencing.

There are seven species of deer in Britain but, in most areas, the smallest native species, the roe deer (*Capreolus capreolus*) and the smallest introduced species, the Asian muntjac (*Muntiacus reevesi*), are the two that can be troublesome in gardens. They feed on a wide range of garden plants and may damage lawns, fences and hedges. The only sure way to keep them out is by using purpose-made 2m-high deer fencing.

Take your interest in mammals further:

Mammals of Britain and Europe, Macdonald and Barrett (Collins, 1993)
www.britishhedgehogs.org.uk – The British Hedgehog Preservation Society
www.bats.org.uk – Bat Conservation Trust
www.abdn.ac.uk/mammal – The Mammal Society
www.badger.org.uk – Badger Trust
www.wildforms.co.uk, *www.wigglywigglers.co.uk* – suppliers of bat boxes, hedgehog houses, squirrel feeders and dormouse nests

Amphibians and reptiles

Reductions in the overall numbers of amphibians and reptiles in Britain, mainly through loss of habitats, but also in some instances because of disease, has meant that gardens have become extremely important alternative habitats, especially for amphibians such as frogs, toads, and newts.

Our British reptile and amphibian fauna is minute on a global scale – we have only three species of snake, three or four lizards, three newts, two toads and around half a dozen species of frog, some of them introduced. But perhaps it's because of this paucity of species that we find them collectively so fascinating.

Although they are generally grouped together, reptiles and amphibians differ in a number of important ways, most obviously in that amphibians require water in which to lay their eggs or spawn. These hatch into larval forms (tadpoles) significantly different from the adults and pass through a state of metamorphosis in order to mature. Although some reptiles live at least partially in water – the familiar grass snake (*Natrix natrix*) is highly aquatic and feeds on amphibians and fish – none breed there and their eggs are laid in warm moist places on land (like garden compost bins) and give rise to young that are essentially miniatures of their parents.

Below Grass snakes are usually easily identifiable by a yellow or orange ring around the neck.

Snakes

As a group, reptiles are relatively rare in gardens and you will certainly be fortunate to see any in an inner city plot. Of the snakes, the smooth snake (*Coronella austriaca*) is confined to sandy areas of the New Forest, parts of Dorset and northern Surrey and it's highly unlikely to be seen in any garden, even there. The adder (*Vipera berus*), our only poisonous species, is much more common in the country at large but is most intolerant of human interference and, despite the understandable fears of many gardeners, is extremely unlikely to occur in gardens.

In practice, any snake found in a garden is almost certain to be a grass snake. I see one or two in my own garden each year and their identity can usually be confirmed by the presence of a yellow or sometimes orange ring around the neck.

Lizards

Among the lizards, the beautiful sand lizard (*Lacerta agilis*) occurs in similar areas to the smooth snake and is also unlikely to be seen in a garden. The common or viviparous lizard (*Lacerta vivipara*) is much more common and may be seen in warm sunny gardens, especially in the south. Conversely there are large areas of the country, as for example across central England, where they are infrequent.

The most common garden lizard by far and also the most common garden reptile is the slow worm (*Anguis fragilis*) although it is atypical among lizards in being legless - and in consequence is often mistaken for a small, bronze coloured snake. They are found in gardens partly because they are the most tolerant of all British reptiles of the presence of humans and also because their preferred food is slugs.

In an area where reptiles are uncommon there is little you can do to entice any into your garden. In districts where they have been seen, however, maintaining undisturbed compost piles or heaps (quite separate from compost bins used for recycling, see p.202) is an extremely valuable practice, as these will provide both slow worms and grass snakes with hibernation and possibly breeding places.

If you have been fortunate enough to see viviparous lizards in your garden, be sure to keep some sunny spots relatively clear of vegetation and ideally with several large rocks that will warm up readily. Lizards love such places in which to bask and catch insects and spiders - they are among the few creatures that are more likely to seen when the ground is bare and exposed.

Above The common or viviparous lizard is relatively common in warm gardens, especially in the south of England, where it may be seen on bare, exposed ground.

Above The palmate newt is commoner than the smooth newt in Scotland but absent from much of central England.
Right Toads outnumber frogs but they are shy creatures and so are less often seen.

Frogs, toads and newts

The common frog (*Rana temporaria*) is appropriately enough the most commonly seen amphibian overall although they are probably outnumbered by the much more secretive toad (*Bufo bufo*). Other species, such as the edible frog (*Rana esculenta*), marsh frog (*Rana ridibunda*) and natterjack toad (*Bufo calamita*) have a much more local distribution and even where they do occur, you are more likely to hear than to see them.

Although there are three native species of newt, they aren't always easy to distinguish. The two most common species, the smooth newt (*Triturus vulgaris*) and the palmate newt (*Triturus helveticus*), are especially tricky and most readily identified by their rather different distribution. The third species is the largest and most handsome of all British amphibians: the great crested newt (*Triturus cristatus*). If you have these creatures in your garden, you will not only be very fortunate but probably also the owner of a very large pond full of aquatic plants.

If you know of a local farm or other pond with an amphibian population, you may be tempted to catch some for your garden. I would discourage you from this. Great crested newts have legal protection and must not be disturbed. Neither should frogs be transferred from wild ponds into garden ponds because of the risk of spreading a serious and lethal disease called red leg - and by similar token, nor should any animals or excess frog spawn be taken in the opposite direction.

By moving animals into an unsuitable habitat, you could even be committing an offence under a little appreciated but important piece of legislation, The Abandonment of Animals Act, 1960.

Grass snakes will be attracted to garden ponds and of course a pond is essential for encouraging amphibians to breed although frogs and toads may be seen among damp, shaded vegetation in any garden. Later in the book, I discuss the management of garden ponds for wildlife (*see pp.180–193*) although the best-laid plans of gardeners aren't always heeded by wild animals. The widely accepted theory is that undisturbed ponds with plenty of native vegetation and no fish are most effective for encouraging amphibians to breed. This was, however, belied in my own garden for many years when the straight-sided formal water lily pond, stocked with goldfish and golden orfe and with an ornamental fountain consistently proved to have a higher and more successful breeding population of both frogs and newts than the pond I had constructed with a series of ledges and carefully stocked with native plants.

Protecting amphibians

Whatever type of garden or pond you have, it is essential to have some form of escape ramp that amphibians can use to crawl out. Formal ponds with overhanging edges offer no means of escape and are quite literally lethal.

I have mentioned that frogs will hide among long grass and, for this reason, special care must be taken when cutting it if a massacre isn't to ensue. Even though I cut long grass with a relatively noisy long-handled hedge trimmer (*see p.162*) and most gardeners use a strimmer or other powered equipment, frogs seem oblivious to the noise and stay motionless until it is too late. I find it helps, therefore, to beat the grass or disturb it in some way before doing the actual cutting.

For more about reptiles and amphibians:

Reptiles and Amphibians of Britain and Europe, Arnold and Ovenden (Collins, 2002)

www.froglife.org – national conservation charity for all reptiles and amphibians

www.herpconstrust.org.uk – The Herpetological Conservation Trust

www.defra.gov.uk/animalh/welfare/domestic – for details of the Abandonment of Animals Act, 1960

Insects and other invertebrates

Of the many thousands of insects and other invertebrates that exist, even in a modestly sized plot, only a tiny fraction are pests. Therefore the vast majority of this multitude of creatures should be at least conserved and at best positively encouraged because they all have a role in the wider cycle of life.

It is a shame that whilst most gardeners would be happy to see more butterflies, larger moths and dragonflies in their gardens, enthusiasm for encouraging much else is distinctly in short supply. I pointed out a few years ago in my book *Fauna Britannica* that, in terms of interest in small garden creatures, beauty matters: 'There are four butterflies (out of around 60) and five moths (out of around 2,500) on the list of British species protected under the Wildlife and Countryside Act; there are only four other insects (out of around 21,000). There are societies for the conservation of butterflies but they give rather little attention to the larger moths and even less to the minor ones; and no-one seems in the least interested in conserving even the rarest of aphids, lice or fleas.'

Overall needs

Nothing has really changed since I wrote my book, except that the more enterprising suppliers are now offering purpose-made versions of items that serious conservation-minded gardeners have been making themselves for years – like nesting boxes for some wild bee species. Before describing these items, therefore, I should look at the overall needs of invertebrates in relation to gardens.

In one sense, my task is all but impossible because with so many thousands of different kinds of creature,

Left Ladybirds are invaluable in the garden because they control pests such as aphids.

Numbers of butterfly and moth species feeding on specific trees and plants

Food plant	No. of species	Food plant	No. of species
Willow	100	Chickweed	24
Birch	87	Rose	23
Oak	71	Alder	21
Hawthorn	65	Broom	21
Blackthorn	54	Hazel	21
Dock	52	Beech	20
Grasses (generally)	42	Knotgrass	20
Poplar	39	Stinging nettle	19
Bramble	32	Ash	16
Bilberry	30	Lime	16
Heather	30	Honeysuckle	15
Plantain	28	Pine	12
Dandelion	27	Privet	11
Apple	26	Clover	9

you will never be able to satisfy the needs of more than a relative few. Conversely, I could argue that my task is easy because whatever type of garden you have, it will be appealing to something! Surprisingly, there have been very few serious studies of the wildlife of gardens, apart from birds, and certainly little is known of the needs of many insects and other small organisms. What few studies have been made, however, are encouraging in indicating that although larger gardens contained more species, there were no qualitative differences between large and small plots; and nor between suburban and rural gardens. In essence, this means that wherever your garden lies and whatever size it is, it will be good for some wildlife.

My advice in the context of attracting insects therefore is the same as my advice for wildlife gardening in general. Have as wide a variety of plants as possible, whether native or exotic, try to have plants that flower and seed at different times of the year and, if possible, try to have at least some parts of your garden that are a little more unkempt. If you are able to set aside a special area for wildlife, you have more options (*see p.153*) and probably more scope for attracting at least some of the less common invertebrates – those most in need of conservation.

Although it is rather a simplistic approach, I have extracted details from the fairly well-known information available about butterfly and moth food plant preferences to offer a list of the native plants that are most likely to attract a wide range of insects in these two groups, with a hint that they may be those with a wide general appeal to insects, too (*see above*).

Choosing plants

Trees and shrubs are crucial as food plants, so choose carefully and select something with good insect appeal. Of course, some insect species are regional in their distribution and you will never attract more than a small proportion of the total – but this can still make an important contribution towards their conservation.

Don't be misled into thinking that the need for grasses can be met by having a normal lawn. Lawn turf is composed of a limited range of mainly hybrid grasses and you need several native grass species to attract the many fascinating creatures that feed on grass, something that can really only be achieved in a dedicated wildlife garden (*see also p.157*).

Nesting sites

It is only recently that the idea of attracting insects in ways other than by growing plants has come to the attention of gardeners. The use of devices that provide insects with nesting or hibernation sites is a valuable additional practice and among those readily obtainable are packs of small tubes to attract red and blue mason bees, larger boxes for bumble bees, and hibernation boxes for ladybirds, butterflies and lacewings.

In my experience, the mason bee nesting boxes are by far the most successful; and in reality, it seems that the insects need little encouraging – I find that mason bees quickly locate and nest in the boxes designed for ladybird hibernation!

Any bundle of small tubes – such as short lengths of hollow bamboo cane of different diameters – will attract them and a considerable number of other insects, too, by mimicking the broken ends of old bramble stems and other hedgerow vegetation.

The bees obligingly indicate when individual tubes have been used by sealing the ends with mud after their eggs have been laid inside. Bumble bee boxes are intended to attract queen bees emerging from hibernation and seeking a nesting site. Bumble bees are hugely important pollinating species because they

Above In searching for pollen bees are attracted to brightly coloured flowers. **Right** Hibernation boxes for ladybirds are now sold at most garden centres. **Below** Old logs are essential for providing shelter for small creatures.

visit a wide range of plants and have hairy bodies that very effectively trap pollen. Yet they seem less adept or willing to adopt artificial boxes. Manufacturers suggest catching a queen bee in early spring to show it the way.

I have mentioned the importance of old logs and large rocks for garden wildlife and they are invaluable for many kinds of insects and other invertebrates that hide and/or nest beneath them. Beetles, centipedes, millipedes, pseudoscorpions, ants, small species of snail, slug and woodlice (including some rare and unusual species that aren't garden pests) are among the creatures that will benefit. You should resist the temptation to keep looking to see what you can find! Lifting the log occasionally is permissible but it should immediately and carefully be replaced in the same position.

Ponds for dragonflies and damsel flies

Dragonflies and their smaller relatives damsel flies never fail to appeal for their size, dramatic appearance, colour and activities. They are large, spectacular and most importantly, they are day-flying. Like so many other wild creatures, their numbers have declined greatly in recent years through the loss of wetland habits and gardens can play a part in helping. Dragonflies are never found far from water in which their eggs are laid and where the immature forms live so a garden pond, as large as possible, is essential to attract them (*see also pp.180–193* for more on ponds).

Above The summer-flowering *Buddleja alternifolia* is not quite as appealing to butterflies as *Buddleja davidii* but it is still a wonderful nectar plant.
Below The vivid colours of damsel flies make them particularly attractive – but you need a pond to lure them into the garden.

To find out more about insects and other invertebrates, check out the following:

Insects, Bob Gibbons (Collins, 2004)
Butterflies and Moths, John Still (Collins, 2005)
www.buglife.org.uk – The Invertebrate Conservation Trust
www.butterfly-conservation.org – also includes moths
www.royensoc.co.uk – Royal Entomological Society
www.wigglywigglers.co.uk, www.wildforms.co.uk – for bug boxes and bricks, insect observatories, bee nesters and ladybird houses

Mosses, liverworts and ferns

Mosses and their close relatives, liverworts, are among the most fascinating and beautiful of all plants, albeit small ones. Add another group of fairly primitive (and rather larger) types, the ferns, and you have an assembly of attractive and extremely important plants many of which are seriously threatened in the wild.

Of all the beautiful types of plant life that gardeners most fail to appreciate, mosses must top the list. Mention moss to almost any gardener and they will conjure up a vision of a less than perfect lawn, a slippery path or 'something' growing on the roof. Mosses are often not even recognised as plants.

In reality, mosses enhance your garden and provide important miniature habitats for a wide range of tiny creatures; as well as food for some larger ones. Huge numbers of tiny beetles and other small insects, mites, woodlice and other invertebrates live on and among moss tufts, some of them feeding on the moss itself, some feeding on each other. And even more creatures use the damp, undisturbed conditions in which to lay their eggs. Birds will often be seen pecking over moss colonies looking for animal life inside and many species use the moss itself as nesting material. Some, like long-tailed tits, build their nests almost entirely of moss.

Moss colonies

There are around 750 species of moss in Britain and about 300 liverworts. None of them is individually very big - the tallest species of moss, the common haircap moss (*Polytrichum commune*), can reach a height of 40cm, although that is an exception. Nonetheless, they grow in colonies and a single clump of a moss, like the common and beautiful woodland species *Leucobryum glaucum*, in

Left Damp-loving moss has colonised this north-facing dry stone wall.

Above Mosses thrive undisturbed on an old roof, providing an important habitat for a wide range of creatures.

which each plant is minute, can be almost 2m in diameter and contain many thousands of individuals. When clumps merge, as they often do in damp woodlands, the entire floor can be covered with a dense velvet carpet. In some Oriental gardens, moss 'lawns' are encouraged. They look magnificent but their cultivation is a lengthy and laborious process and not one I suggest you try.

Although you need a magnifying lens to appreciate the details of their beauty and structure, mosses have tiny, simple, very delicate leaves. Many look like miniature Christmas trees but there is a wide variety of form. Some species that cause lawn perfectionists so much heartache have their minute leaves compressed against the stems, giving them an almost rope-like appearance – these are called thread mosses.

Bog mosses

. . . .

A quite distinct, remarkably beautiful but also remarkably threatened group of mosses are the bog mosses belonging to the genus *Sphagnum*. The name

sphagnum may be familiar in another gardening context – long-dead sphagnum moss is the major constituent of some types of peat. The use of peat in gardens is also unsupportable because the bogs from which it is dug are threatened and fragile habitats. The sphagnum in the peat may be dead but many other organisms live in and on the remains (*see p.84*).

In addition to lawns, you will find mosses anywhere that soil is left undisturbed – on the surfaces of beds and borders that haven't been hoed or dug, under trees, especially if the soil isn't too dry, on roof tiles, large stones and walls where tiny soil particles accumulate, and at the edges of paths where no-one walks. They are also extremely common on tree bark, especially on the shaded side of trees. The damper and rougher the bark, the more luxuriant their growth will be. Undisturbed fallen logs are also an extremely rich habitat for them.

Types of liverwort

There are two main types of liverwort. The first group, the leafy liverworts, are extremely small and extremely fragile. Many of them grow in the same places as mosses although their fragile nature means they are even more dependent on dampness and are quite intolerant of drying out.

If you carefully pull out a small tangle of dead vegetation from the soil surface in an undisturbed area of your garden and tease apart the old plant stems and leaves, you will probably find some. Even I can't pretend they will make a particularly impressive display in the wider context of your garden but they do emphasise the importance of not being too scrupulous in clearing away garden 'debris'. In the cause of tidiness, you could be wiping out a multitude of tiny ecosystems.

The species in the second group of liverworts are much larger. They are called thallose liverworts – a thallus is a simply a lump of plant growth, a bit like a seaweed, with no roots and no special tissues for carrying water and food. You will find them growing on the mud or rocks at the edges of streams and lakes. They are also common on the compost of plant pots that have been left undisturbed for two or three years

All mosses and liverworts reproduce by spores, not flowers, and the appearance of the tiny, spore-bearing structures is a large part of their appeal as they sprout like a small forest of miniature pin-heads. These are often green, but sometimes brown, orange or even bright red and it is at this point that they can be particularly striking. Raising moss and liverwort plants artificially by sowing spores isn't easy, however, and encouraging them into your garden is essentially dependent on encouraging the micro-habitats in which they will grow naturally.

Native ferns

Ferns are generally better known and much better appreciated than mosses and liverworts because most are larger – some a great deal larger. The largest native

Fern reproduction

Ferns reproduce by spores and the rough brown patches you may find beneath their fronds, often in regular and characteristic patterns, are the spore-bearing structures. It is possible to buy fern spores, of both native and exotic species. They look like dust and are a little more tricky than most seeds to germinate. But while raising ferns in this way is a fascinating exercise, it doesn't really play a part in wildlife gardening. Allowing naturally wind-blown spores to select their own place to germinate and grow is more appropriate – as well as far simpler.

Above A few ferns can tolerate the dry
tops of walls.
Left Liverworts are very fragile plants that
need damp conditions to survive.

British fern species, the magnificent royal fern
(*Osmunda regalis*), can grow to 2m tall, so you are
hardly likely to overlook it. Many of the larger species
of fern, native and exotic, are widely grown as garden
plants. Although one fern species, bracken (*Pteridium
aquilinum*) is a serious and invasive weed and a number
of others are too large to be allowed to self-sow, there
are nonetheless numerous small and extremely
beautiful species that will appear naturally, especially
in damp, shady corners and crevices where they should
be left to grow and develop.

Among the most beautiful and welcome of native
ferns are the delicate species of *Asplenium*, often
called maidenhair ferns, which colonise crevices in
undisturbed damp walls. Another common species is

the dainty little parsley fern (*Cryptogramma crispa*)
which is frequently seen on walls built from acidic rocks
like granite, and will be found in many gardens in the
west of the country.

Probably the most common native fern, however, is
one of the few British species with undivided fronds, the
hart's tongue fern (*Phyllitis scolopendrium*). It will grow
in almost any damp, shady corner and it was the first
fern to colonise the inner wall of my garden well when
I fitted a glass cover. It is still the main species there
although it has since been joined by one of the
maidenhair ferns.

It's important to remember that mosses, liverworts
and ferns require an undisturbed habitat. It takes about
two years from the initial germination of a spore to the
appearance of something resembling a plant and in
that time, a trowel, hoe, broom, jet washer or path
disinfectant can so easily bring it all to a premature end.

Fungi and lichens

Mushrooms and toadstools have a very distinct appeal. Some are rare and incredibly beautiful, others more common and ordinary-looking – but all are fascinating. Lichens are part fungus and part alga, and like fungi, are well worth encouraging in the garden – what you will need is plenty of patience.

Few gardeners will want to encourage microscopic fungi in their gardens, principally because a large number of them cause plant diseases. Sadly, mushrooms and toadstools have become collectively tarred with the brush of looking vaguely like the tree and shrub pathogen honey fungus (*Armillaria mellea*) or of being thought poisonous, dangerous and a threat to life. None of these things should be of concern. Honey fungus isn't nearly as common as is often believed and it does have a characteristic and fairly distinctive appearance.

Most garden toadstools aren't honey fungus and whilst a very few kinds certainly are poisonous, so are many garden plants and it should be no deterrent to encouraging them to grow in the garden unless you have young children with a propensity for eating anything they find.

Leaving areas undisturbed

As with mosses and liverworts however, the key word is encouraging because it isn't feasible to sow or plant toadstools and imagine they will grow. And similarly, although perhaps even more importantly, the secret of success is to leave areas undisturbed. The mushrooms and toadstools that appear above ground are simply the spore-producing bodies of microscopic mould threads

or mycelium in the soil. It is usually only after several years of unhindered development that the toadstools appear and this is why you will seldom see them in vegetable gardens or in ornamental beds that are regularly dug and hoed.

Perhaps the most common exceptions to this rule and two species that do thrive on disturbed soil in garden beds are two of the most impressive. The stinkhorn (*Phallus impudicus*) is so distinctive, both

Right The blusher (*Amanita rubescens*) is a common toadstool in undisturbed soil beneath trees.

in its appearance and its odour, that is unlikely to be forgotten or mistaken for anything else. By contrast, the parasol mushroom (*Macrolepiota rhacods*) is simply imposing; one of the largest and most beautiful of all British fungi. Elsewhere in the garden, if it is feasible to leave areas of soil undisturbed, you should do so. Relatively damp conditions beneath trees with a natural carpet of leaf mould are areas that are most likely to produce something.

Many of the fungi that appear on the soil close to particular types of plant, especially beneath particular trees, do so for a specific reason. Their subterranean threads are closely entangled with the roots of the trees to form what is called a mycorrhiza, a mutually beneficial feeding arrangement for both tree and fungus. But although the fungus will be there for as long as the tree, it may be several years before any of the associated toadstools appear; and like most toadstools, even then they will be erratic and unpredictable in their occurrence. Some of the mushrooms and toadstools that emerge from the soil may in reality be growing on buried plant remains such as pieces of old wood and in a woodland, fallen logs are always rich hunting grounds. The possibility of encouraging a wide range of wood-decaying toadstools is yet another reason for having a collection of old logs, preferably of deciduous trees, somewhere in any dedicated wildlife area although it is less practicable in a more conventional garden.

One particularly rich and interesting hunting ground for garden fungi is on the bark and wood chip mulches that have become so popular in gardens in recent years. Nearly 200 species of mushroom and toadstool have been found growing on wood chip mulch and using these mulches gives you the opportunity to see a wide range of interesting fungi in your garden that otherwise would only occur in woodland. Although it is a much more expensive way of mulching your beds than by using home-produced compost or leaf mould, using it on a small area can pay fascinating wildlife dividends.

Perhaps the most familiar place in a garden to find fungi is on the lawn, where numerous small, generally

Above Mushrooms growing in a ring, often called a fairy ring, can occur on any large expanse of grass.

brown-coloured toadstools are very common, especially in autumn. They are quite harmless to the lawn turf and when gardeners take the trouble to examine them closely, they will find them fascinating, even beautiful. The fact that most lawns are dosed from time to time with fertiliser will always limit the number of species that grow, although – interestingly – lawn-mowing does not in itself discourage them. It mimics the grazing of animals and if lawns are left unmown, some fungi will disappear although other kinds may take their place.

Waxcap lawns

Given patience, luck and a large enough area of mown turf that can be set aside for the purpose, it may be possible to encourage the development of one of the most fascinating, rare and valuable of all wildlife habitats – a waxcap lawn.

The waxcaps are a group of distinctive, often brightly coloured toadstools, mostly with narrowly conical caps and a glossy, waxy appearance. They grow in undisturbed, close-cropped turf and, although from a newly seeded

Above Crustose lichens typically encrust undisturbed stone walls.

lawn it may be feasible to encourage possibly one or two species in a decade, it would be a slow process to obtain a full colour range of the more attractive, rare types.

It is much better to change the management of an existing lawn. Stop using artificial fertilisers, moss killers and lime – the presence of some moss is always an indication of a potentially good waxcap lawn. Keep mowing the law and removing clippings until early autumn when the toadstools may begin to appear.

It's impossible to predict how long after the cessation of fertiliser and moss killer application waxcaps might be seen. You might expect the more common species, such as snowy waxcap (*Hygrocybe*

virginea) and blackening waxcap (*Hygrocybe conica*) within 10 years; more sensitive species, like splendid waxcap (*Hygrocybe splendidissima*) could take more than 30 years to develop.

It's quite acceptable to walk on a waxcap lawn and use it recreationally in the same way as usual; oddly enough, some trampling is even thought to be beneficial to certain groups of fungi, like the earth-tongues, species of *Geoglossum*. Overall, the conclusion seems to be that looking after and encouraging a waxcap lawn is a good deal less work than trying to destroy it!

Types of lichen

Lichens are generally considered at the same time as fungi, for the logical reason that every lichen is half fungus! They are unique in being dual organisms, part fungus and part alga living entwined together.

There are several different kinds of lichen but they are most simply divided into three main groups: the leafy, leathery foliose kinds; the many branched, miniature shrub-like fruticose kinds; and the hard, scab-like crustose lichens. Foliose lichens are most likely to be seen on neglected lawns on poor soils, provided the grass is cut fairly short. The dog lichen is the most common species. Fruticose lichens are the characteristic lichens of moorland and wet, mild woodlands where they can be astonishingly lush and beautiful; in gardens, you are only likely to see the more modest species growing on old wooden fences and gateposts. Crustose lichens are the typical lichens of gravestones and old, undisturbed stone walls.

Encouraging lichens

Gardening books offer recipes for encouraging lichens to grow on stone and other walling materials by the expedient of painting the surface with cow manure or yoghurt, or both. I have done it and think it probably does speed up the process but the main watchword for encouraging lichens in the garden is patience.

Yoghurt pots
Mix together equal volumes of yoghurt and runny cow manure [1]. Paint it on the outside of your container – the rougher the surface, the better the mixture will stick [2]. In time, the rain will wash off the excess, and lichens and even mosses may establish. Although it isn't guaranteed to work, I do think it helps [3].

> **Identifying mushrooms**
>
> Although there are many good field guides to help in the identification of mushrooms and toadstools, never collect any to eat unless an expert checks their identity. See the website of the British Mycological Society: *www.britmycolsoc.org.uk*

MANAGING HABITATS IN YOUR GARDEN

In this section of the book, I look at the different elements of the average garden, including flower beds and borders, hedges, trees, shrubberies, lawns, and areas of hard landscaping and explain how best to manage them for the benefit of wildlife. Every garden, no matter how formal, can be organised in a wildlife-friendly way.

For every gardener, the word garden conjures up something different. No two gardens are the same and you only need take a walk around one of the suburban post-war housing estates where identical houses follow each other for road after road in serried ranks to realise that everyone's garden is individual. In truth, the way that every gardener interprets differently the possibilities from identical plots is utterly fascinating, saying as much about human nature as horticulture. I can't give a single blueprint, therefore, that will fit every option and describe the way each and every garden can be managed in a wildlife-friendly way. What I can do is to look at the range of features and elements that make up a typical garden and see how each can be used to best effect; but first I hope I can encourage you to look at your garden in its entirety to see if you have the most wildlife-friendly balance.

More variety, more wildlife

Overall, the greater the variety of plants, the greater will be the variety of wildlife you attract. It doesn't take much to work out that a lawn, which contains a handful of grass species plus a few interloping weeds, is likely to contain a pretty depauperate fauna. That isn't to say the fauna won't include some interesting, important and perhaps rare species; but if your garden doesn't have much else except lawn, your contribution to biodiversity overall will be limited.

The other extreme in a normal, typical garden is probably a perennial border containing a mixture of woody shrubs and herbaceous plants. This will be relatively rich in wildlife although it will be wildlife that tolerates or is oblivious to the changes that come about in autumn when herbaceous plants die down and are cleared away and leaves fall from deciduous

Above The evergreen shrub *Berberis darwinii* not only looks beautiful in the garden but its orange flowers in spring and berries in autumn will also benefit wildlife.

shrubs. In between these two extremes are such interesting areas as annual beds, vegetable gardens and containers. Here the range of plants is limited – very limited in containers – while the changes at the end of the season are catastrophic – the plants disappear and the soil is subject to what amounts to a minor earthquake as spade, fork, manure and compost cause wholesale upheaval.

The ideal habitat for wildlife in a normal garden therefore might logically be satisfied by a mixed planting of species that changes a little during the course of the season, but not hugely. A shrubbery is one option but the number of individual plants is likely to be small in the space that is available in most modern gardens. I think therefore such an area is best satisfied by a mixed hedge, ideally containing a significant proportion of native species. Clearly, you can't have a garden composed entirely of hedge but if – perish the thought – I was asked to introduce a legal requirement for gardeners to follow in the cause of helping our national biodiversity, it would be to make the planting and possession of a least a few metres of mixed native hedge compulsory!

Above One of the formal areas of the author's garden. Every garden will have scope for some wildlife merit.

Flower beds and borders

All except the smallest gardens have space for a flower bed or border of some kind and they can provide the most marvellous opportunities for encouraging and assisting wildlife, especially insects and birds. A mixture of plants is generally better for wildlife than plantings made up of one type of plant only.

In modern gardens, there's often no real difference between a bed and a border although originally a border was literally just that: a planted area that bordered something - a lawn, a boundary or a path, for example. By contrast, a bed stood alone in the midst of other types of planting. Sometimes 'bed' now refers to an area that contains predominantly one type of ornamental plant – an annual flower bed for example – by contrast with a border which contains a mixture. This seems an appropriate point, therefore, to explain why, in wildlife gardening, mixtures are generally better than what are known as monocultures - plantings made up of one type of plant only.

Although the flowers, foliage or other parts of some plants are attractive to a wide range of insects, others appeal to only a few. If you have created a large planting of a type of plant that happens to appeal to only one or two kinds of insect, therefore, your garden wildlife will be fairly limited. But it's simply not reasonable to expect gardeners to investigate the wildlife appeal of every plant they intend to grow. It's easier to have a wide range.

Prolonging flowering

And instead of relying solely on types of plant that individually flower over a long period, choose not only a wide variety but a wide variety that collectively give flowers for the longest proportion of the season. In a mixed border containing bulbs, annuals, perennials and shrubs, you have the best possible opportunity to do this. Shrubs are the best bet for winter flowers, followed by

some evergreen perennials. In early spring, bulbs and some kinds of herbaceous perennials add to the variety, followed as summer arrives by annuals and more perennials. Even varying the colour of your plants will help - although insects 'see' flowers differently from us, it's clear that reds and blues have a separate and distinct appeal from yellows and oranges. If you must have plants of only one colour, orange or yellow will usually appeal to the widest range of insect species. For this reason, a few orange or yellow flowers among your vegetables may attract hoverflies and other beneficial insects that feed on aphids.

Beneficial flower shapes

The shapes of flowers help, too. Many exotic flowers, especially many half-hardy annuals, originate in tropical climates where they evolved long tubular blooms to be pollinated by humming birds with their elongated beaks and tongues. The tongues of British bumble bees may not be long enough to reach the nectar, while honey bees, which have even shorter tongues, fare worse still. It's important therefore to include a proportion of plants that are derived from British, European or at least temperate climate species (*see p.86*).

Above right A flower garden planted with wildlife in mind, featuring a diverse range of flowering plants.
Below right Late summer colour in the herbaceous border – yellows and oranges are particularly appealing to insects.

Above left *Rudbeckia* 'Cherokee Sunset' is an excellent annual for late-season insect attraction.
Above right *Viola tricolor* is a reliable all-year-round annual.

The importance of shrubs

Shrubs have a particular role to play in wildlife gardening, both in a dedicated shrubbery and in a mixed border. Their above-ground framework is permanent, a huge advantage in that they don't have to begin 'from nothing' each season and so can produce leaves and flowers as soon as the temperature and day length are appropriate for each species.

But they provide all-year round shelter, too, and in a mixed border, small creatures can spend the winter in or underneath shrubs and then move rapidly onto the newly emerging foliage and flowers of neighbouring plants – although we should always accept that this can be as true for unwelcome pests as for desirable wildlife.

A similar advantage is conferred by a border – in the traditional sense of being alongside some other feature. A fence, wall or hedge adjoining a border confers added shelter where wildlife can hide or even hibernate in readiness for the return of flowers and foliage in the spring.

Annuals

Annual plants are those that complete their entire life cycle from seed to seed in the course of a single season. A number of vegetables, such as lettuces and beetroot, fall into this category, although many other common vegetables are in fact biennials. They are harvested in their first year but, if left, would continue growing to flower in the second season. Most garden brassicas, like cabbages and Brussels sprouts, are biennials. Many gardeners will have seen the yellow flowers of those left in the ground into the second year after their harvest time (*see p.116*). In the flower garden, however, while there are a number of genuine annuals and also a few biennials, like sweet Williams (*Dianthus barbatus*) and wallflowers (*Erysimum*), a large proportion of the plants we call annuals and grow for one season only are actually tender perennials from warmer climates – they will live for many years in their native habitats but they can't do so in Britain because they are killed by the autumn frosts.

Although so many 'annual flowers' do originate in exotic climates – a large number, for example, in South Africa – this doesn't necessarily mean they have no appeal for British wildlife. You only need look at pelargoniums, petunias, tagetes and other summer delights to see that butterflies, bees and many other insects visit them regularly. Nonetheless, visiting doesn't necessarily mean benefiting – there are many annual flowers whose nectar (and pollen) is simply inaccessible to British insects.

Research has shown that, just as with perennials (*see p.90*), the elongated flowers of some annuals can't be reached by native insects. Interestingly, some flowers (both native and exotic) that are elongated but not excessively so can be preferentially beneficial to long-tongued bumble bees, many species of which are becoming rare. These bees can reach the nectar whereas honey bees can't. Research has also revealed that some double-flowered annuals may be particularly useless for wildlife generally and insects especially.

Double flowers usually arise when some or all of the stamens are converted to petals. They can't therefore produce pollen (that's why they are beneficial to hay fever sufferers) and many produce no nectar. Given that they don't produce any seeds either, plants such as double-flowered petunias are good examples of summer annuals that have almost no wildlife benefit – apart from possibly enhancing the population of some aphids and therefore being of slight interest to insect-eating birds! In practice, rather few annual flowers produce seeds – sunflowers are particularly graphic

Right Sunflowers are imposing annuals that appeal to many insects, especially bees, and produce seeds for birds and other creatures, too.

Above Annuals in containers bring
colour and wildlife appeal to bare areas.
Left Single flowers are best for
pollinating insects.

and important exceptions – but a balance is needed in the care of those that do: a balance between clearing them away as soon as they begin to look unattractive at the end of summer and leaving them long enough for birds to take advantage of the seeds as food supplies grow short in early winter. As I have said many times, wildlife gardening is compromise gardening.

Mixing exotic and native annuals

For wildlife value in annuals therefore, always mix the exotic with the native and the commonplace – or at least, garden varieties derived from them. A particular value of annuals is that they give results quickly and enable you almost to respond to changing circumstances. Using quick-growing annual flowers offers an excellent way of providing both colour and wildlife appeal to borders or other long-term plantings in the early years, before the slower-growing perennials

and shrubs have filled the available space. It's often said that nature abhors a vacuum and if you don't fill the gaps with something, nature will. Weeds will colonise the holes and although in consequence you will have some flowers in your borders and some wildlife will accompany them, the results may not look particularly attractive. The smaller the garden, the greater any effects are magnified, and in limited space, it is especially important to choose annuals that have the colour, structure and fragrance to offer something worthwhile.

In most gardens, annuals probably achieve their greatest benefit in containers. Whether in hanging baskets, window boxes or tubs, they bring colour and interest – often close to the house – where otherwise there would be none. Choosing colours, flower shapes and forms that are attractive to pollinating insects also applies here, although even the most dedicated wildlife enthusiast may not want hordes of buzzing bees near the windows or next to the family's outdoor dining area. There is some argument, therefore, for choosing flowers like double petunias here simply because they are *less* likely to attract insects.

Perennials

Although the huge border of herbaceous perennials is a thing of the past in all except the largest and grandest of gardens, perennial flowers are still highly important components in most. The fact that the perennials sections in most garden centres are generally second in size only to those of shrubs reflects this. And just as they are important garden features so they are, or should be, important wildlife features, too.

A perennial is a plant that lives for more than two years and is usually capable of flowering every season. Perennials are sometimes called herbaceous perennials to emphasise that they don't have any permanent woody framework and so distinguish them from shrubs, which do. The boundaries are a bit blurred, however, and plants like fuchsias, penstemons, vincas and the lovely blue-flowered *Ceratostigma* have a foot in both camps.

Moreover, whilst the traditional perception of a perennial is of a plant that loses its leaves in autumn and more or less dies down to soil level, there are many exceptions to this; plants that are most conveniently called evergreen perennials and retain foliage all year round. Sometimes the individual leaves persist for many years while in other instances, they are renewed annually, the older foliage dying back after the new leaves have unfolded. Familiar examples of evergreen perennials are kniphofias (red hot pokers), hellebores and phormiums.

However, as I have often told gardeners, being perennial doesn't equate with being immortal and depending on the species, more or less attention is needed if the plants are to continue to develop vigorously and not outgrow their allotted space. Some regular feeding and/or mulching is desirable, and periodic lifting and dividing may also be necessary.

Above *Helleborus foetidus* will continue for many years without being lifted or divided.
Left *Lysimachia punctata* is another easy-to-grow perennial that is attractive to insects.
Above right A mixed border of annuals with a few perennials and plenty of wildlife appeal.

Many kinds of cultivated *Primula* for example must be divided every two years to retain their vigour, whereas native primroses (*Primula vulgaris*) will self-seed and spread without any attention. Similarly, the so-called Christmas rose (*Helleborus niger*) is rather a fussy plant, needing minimal competition from other species, cutting back of old foliage and even some cosseting of the large delicate flowers. By contrast, related hellebores, including the native *Helleborus foetidus* but also exotics like the Lenten rose (*Helleborus x hybridus*) will continue for many seasons without interference.

These factors should be borne in mind when selecting perennials for their wildlife merit. In borders where aesthetic appearance and tidiness are likely to be priorities and where regular feeding, mulching, lifting and dividing will take place, there is no real merit in selecting plants that can just as easily be left to their own devices. They can be chosen for less formal parts of the garden, such as 'wilder' areas beneath trees. Among evergreen perennials are a small number of species that have winter interest and appeal, both for

us and for wildlife. The cover of foliage they afford provides shelter and protection while those that flower in the winter may be appreciated by the few insects that are routinely flying at that time of the year or, more commonly, have been tricked into activity by an abnormal spell of mild weather.

Some winter flowers like the various species of *Daphne*, have a particularly powerful fragrance, presumably to attract insects from some distance away. By contrast it should also be borne in mind that many winter flowers have no perfume because they are designed for wind pollination.

Much of what I have said about annuals in relation to wildlife applies to perennials too; most especially the fact that some long-tubed flowers are inaccessible to bees and that double-flowered forms have extremely limited value (*see p.87*). With no pollen and often no nectar, double flowers have nothing to offer pollinating insects. And being unable to produce seeds, they have no merit as bird food when colder weather arrives in late autumn.

Border perennials with wildlife appeal, especially for bees, butterflies and other insects

Name	Description
Anthemis	Medium-sized clump-forming plants, some suitable for ground cover. Feathery, finely dissected leaves and daisy-like flowers, which are yellow or white with yellow centres. Require free-draining light sandy soil in full sun or partial shade. Intolerant of damp, cold situations
Bear's breeches (*Acanthus*)	Large, coarse but attractive semi-evergreen plants for the back of the border. Glossy, prickly leaves and very striking tall spikes of white, pink or mauve flowers
Elephant's ears [1] (*Bergenia*)	Medium-sized evergreen, good ground cover in borders or shaded shrubberies. Rosettes of leathery, glossy, green leaves, sometimes flushed red in autumn and clusters of bell-shaped flowers in white or shades of pink, red or violet, in spring. An unusual flower colour for early in the year
Geraniums/cranesbills [2]	Perhaps the best of all herbaceous perennials, their value limited only by the restricted colour range and short flowering season of individual varieties although collectively, they offer flowers through the summer. Lobed leaves, round or pointed, often aromatic, sometimes colouring well in autumn. Saucer-shaped or star-shaped flowers are pink, white, blue, or purple, solitary or in clusters, from spring to early autumn
Golden alyssum/basket of gold (*Aurinia saxatilis*)	This plant has simple green, grey or silvery grey leaves. Masses of small vivid yellow flowers are produced in late spring
Granny's bonnet [3] (*Aquilegia vulgaris*)	Relatively large, many-lobed, light green to greyish green leaves. Funnel-shaped flowers, most with prominent spurs arising from each of the five petals. A much-loved old cottage garden plant with deep red, blue, purple, and red-purple flowers, occasionally pink or white, in early summer
Ice plant [4] (*Sedum spectabile*)	Upright, clump-forming relative of many alpines with fleshy leaves of pale blue-green, pink flowers in early autumn. The best of all perennials for butterflies
Lady's mantle (*Alchemilla mollis*)	Small, herbaceous, low-growing clumps with feathery inflorescences of tiny greenish yellow flowers in summer. Tolerant of most types of soil except very dry or heavy, wet conditions
Lungwort (*Pulmonaria saccharata*)	Clump-forming, evergreen, elliptic, mid-green leaves with white spots or blotches, sometimes almost covering the surface and white, red-violet or violet flowers with dark green calyces from late winter to late spring

Name	Description
Lenten rose [5] (*Helleborus* x *hybridus*)	Very variable plants with leathery, dark green basal leaves and saucer-shaped white to greenish-cream spring flowers
Mallow (*Lavatera rosea*)	Saucer- or funnel-shaped, five-petalled pink or white flowers, sometimes with characteristic dark veining, from midsummer to mid-autumn. Leaves are mainly light green or greyish green, heart-shaped to triangular
Michaelmas daisy [6] (*Aster*)	Daisy-like inflorescences in a variety of colours produced singly or in clusters from summer to autumn. Adored by butterflies
Monkshood [7] (*Aconitum*)	Ideal for the shadier border or woodland garden. Rich green leaves and hooded flowers in shades of dark purple, blue and white borne on flower spikes held well above the leaves. All parts are highly toxic and leaves may cause skin irritation when handled
Oriental poppy (*Papaver orientale*)	Clump-forming, deeply divided, bristly, oblong to lance-shaped mid-green leaves, with vividly coloured, often scarlet flowers, each petal with a bold black blotch at the base, from early to midsummer
Phlox (*Phlox paniculata*)	Dish-shaped to funnel-shaped flowers, with tubular bases opening to five ovate petals, in terminal inflorescences, in summer
Shasta daisy (*Leucanthemum* x *superbum*)	Basal rosettes of dark green, entire, toothed, pinnate leaves with scalloped or lobed edges. Daisy-like, single, semi-double or double white flowers
Sweet bergamot (*Monarda didyma*)	Produces clusters of narrow, tubular, two-lipped usually red flowers surrounded by pointed bracts
Teasel (*Dipsacus fullonum*)	Tall, robust, stiffly bristly plants that produce tiny papery flowers on conical spiny heads in summer
Valerian (*Centranthus ruber*)	Fragrant, small red flowers from late spring to late summer
Winter aconite [8] (*Eranthis hyemalis*)	Small tuberous plant with fairly finely dissected pinnate or palmate-lobed leaves and small, golden-yellow, buttercup-like flowers from midwinter to early spring, generally flowering at the same time as snowdrops
Yarrow (*Achillea millefolium*)	Flattened heads of tiny flowers borne in tightly packed or loose clusters held well above the foliage. Greyish green, fern-like leaves, with a characteristically spicy scent

Autumn seeds

Carefully chosen perennials can be especially valuable in autumn because, unlike half-hardy annuals, they can survive frosts without collapsing. Leave the seedheads in place and keep a regular check on bird feeding activity. Only when the seeds have been exhausted should the dead stems be cleared, shredded and composted. If they are left until the spring, they will not only appear increasingly unsightly but may also harbour diseases. Anyone who has watched garden birds will know that different types of seedhead vary in their overall appeal for particular birds. A classic example of a bird with a predilection for certain seeds is the goldfinch; it is the only species of finch that is able to remove the seeds from teasels by virtue of its rather slender beak. I grow teasels in my borders solely for the pleasure of seeing goldfinches dine on them.

Good perennials for supplying seeds as bird food in autumn

Bear's breeches (*Acanthus spinosus*)	New Zealand flax (*Phormium tenax*)
Bugbane (*Cimicifuga racemosa*)	Orange coneflower (*Rudbeckia fulgida*) **[above right]**
Burning bush (*Dictamnus albus*)	Ornamental onions (*Allium*)
Globe thistle (*Echinops ritro*)	Pincushion flower (*Scabiosa caucasica*)
Ice plant (*Sedum spectabile*)	Purple coneflower (*Echinacea purpurea*)
Lady's mantle (*Alchemilla mollis*)	Russian sage (*Perovskia atriplicifolia*)
Liatris (*Liatris spicata*)	Scotch thistle (*Onopordon acanthium*)
Meadow sweet (*Filipendula ulmaria*)	Teasel (*Dipsacus fullonum*) **[above left]**
Michaelmas daisy (*Aster*)	Yarrow (*Achillea millefolium*)
Monbretia (*Crocosmia*)	Also many kinds of perennial grasses

Managing your border to help wildlife

• Use rustic twiggy supports for at least some of the plants. They will harbour much miniature wildlife in a way that metal plant supports never will. **[1]**

• Tie your plants with degradable garden twine rather than plastic ties that last forever – even when recycled in compost. **[2]**

• Apply plenty of organic mulch to the soil early in the season and so provide a wonderful habitat for a huge range of tiny creatures. If you are fortunate, this might encourage the appearance of some quite fascinating species of mushrooms (*see p.76*). Any kind of mulch will also retain moisture and suppress weeds but biodegradable mulch, whether of garden-made compost, leaf mould or proprietary wood chip, bark, fibre or other material will slowly be drawn into the soil by worms and enrich the soil as it decomposes. **[3]**

• In autumn and early winter, remember the value of seedheads as food for birds (*see p.96*). Don't cut down everything too hastily in the cause of tidiness.

• Bear in mind that many border perennials require regular attention in the form of lifting or dividing and self-evidently, creatures that are intolerant of this disturbance are unlikely to thrive. (For more about choosing perennial flowers, *see p.90*.)

Hedges

Hedges are ancient and often beautiful features of our landscape that have been especially important since the Enclosure Acts of the 18th and early 19th centuries which required the dividing up of land into clearly defined areas. They soon came to provide an important and special habitat for wildlife of many kinds.

In effect, a hedge is a long narrow wood with many-branched shrubs and with a ground flora of low-growing plants that is relatively undisturbed. So important have hedgerows become that many birds are largely dependent on them as nesting sites and a number of animals and plants have acquired the word 'hedge' as a prefix to their name – hedge mustard, hedge parsley, hedge woundwort, hedge sparrow, hedge brown, hedgehog and so on.

The dense habit of plants that make up a hedge also encourages the growth of a number of climbers, such as ivy, white bryony, honeysuckle and bramble, that in turn provide important food for many creatures. Of course, not all the plants and animals that make their homes in hedges are necessarily beneficial. They can act as reservoirs for weeds and weed seeds and provide shelter for many garden pests. But conversely, they also provide important shelter for beneficial insects like ladybirds and hover-flies.

There has been much concern about the removal of hedges from the countryside at large and the loss of these areas that are so important for wildlife. In 1997, legislation was introduced to protect important farm hedgerows in England and Wales but gardeners can do a great deal to help by providing hedges in their gardens, both as boundaries and to divide areas within the garden itself.

Although there are occasions when a fence or wall makes more sense as a garden boundary (*see p.104*) – not least for the fact that it provides almost instant protection and privacy – in the long term, a hedge is more durable, more attractive and immeasurably better as a wildlife habitat. If a fence is a necessary expedient, I always advocate planting a hedge alongside it. The hedge will be reaching a functional size at around the time the fence may be coming to the end of its effective life.

In most aspects of wildlife gardening, variety of planting is the key to success. Hedges are no exception and a mixed planting, including a range of native species as well as some conifers will generally be the most successful. The less important it is that the hedge should provide a robust and impenetrable boundary, the greater can be the assortment of species grown.

Choosing hedge plants

In choosing the types of plant for a hedge, your basic requirements will usually be little different from the needs of wildlife: relatively rapid growth and dense cover. Against that must be set several factors. First, a really dense evergreen hedging plant like Lawson cypress may provide attractive nesting sites for birds but its habit militates against subsidiary vegetation – which is so important for other creatures – from gaining a foothold.

A slower-growing deciduous hedge is more versatile but may not give you adequate screening in winter. Beech, which is deciduous but retains its dead foliage, offers a possible compromise. Moreover, rapid growth means more clipping – fast-growing hedges, unfortunately, don't stop growing when they reach 2m

Above The glossy evergreen leaves of holly make an attractive, impenetrable hedge in which birds like to nest.

in height – and hedge clipping is highly counter-productive to bird nesting. There appear to be no statistics available on how many birds forsake their nests because hedges are clipped too early in the season but the numbers must be considerable.

When to clip

There is no easy answer to the question of when hedges should be clipped. Clipping too early in the year means nesting birds will be disturbed; clipping later may mean the new growth has already become woody and it will be difficult to maintain an attractive appearance.

Flowering hedges, or flowering shrubs used in mixed hedges, create a further problem because if they are clipped early, the flowers will be lost and no fruit will form. If they are clipped later, the fruits themselves will be removed. Only time and experience in your own garden will indicate how best to achieve a compromise but I can't stress too strongly that you should do all you can to check that young birds have left their nests before you begin.

Bearing in mind the importance for wildlife of the ground-cover vegetation beneath a hedge, resist the temptation to clear it away too regularly as you will be destroying the habitats of many creatures, small plants and fungi. Once again, a compromise is needed – between catering for the needs of wildlife whilst not allowing an important garden boundary to be choked with other plants.

Important features of common hedging plants

Hedge	Special feature
Beech **[right]** (*Fagus sylvatica*)	The ideal deciduous hedging plant in many ways, offering all-round screening, through retaining its dead leaves during winter. Its drawbacks are a relatively slow growth rate and a propensity to become infested with beech aphid
Berberis	Fairly fast-growing but not very dense. With the exception of the more vigorous *Berberis* x *stenophylla*, it should not be used where more than about 1.5m in height is needed. The prickles make them useful boundary markers
Blackthorn, plums, sloe (*Prunus* species)	Wild plums and related species tend to be too coarse and open-growing to make satisfactory hedges in small gardens. They are, however, valuable as components of mixed hedges in dedicated wildlife gardens, with their blossom and fruits an added bonus
Box (*Buxus sempervirens*)	The small evergreen leaves of box make it a good hedging plant but it is fairly slow-growing and whilst used by some birds for nesting, has little overall wildlife value. Many forms are highly susceptible to a damaging disease called box blight
Cotoneaster	Two species of cotoneaster are generally sold for hedging purposes: *Cotoneaster lacteus*, an evergreen with large, elliptical evergreen leaves, and *Cotoneaster simonsii*, which is more or less evergreen in most areas but smaller, and with smaller leaves. Both have white flowers and dark red berries, which are valuable for birds
Escallonia	The most common species *Escallonia macrantha* and its varieties make good evergreen and flowering hedges in mild areas, especially by the seaside, but they have no particular wildlife appeal
Flowering currant (*Ribes sanguineum*)	This popular old cottage garden shrub is purely ornamental because its structure is too open to offer any real wildlife value
Forsythia	The various species and hybrids of *Forsythia* offer relatively little screening and are of little wildlife value although the bright yellow flowers are useful for early-season insects
Hawthorn, quickthorn (*Crataegus monogyna*)	Hawthorn has proved its worth over many centuries as a farm boundary fence. It is robust, dense, prickly, stock-proof and most amenable to being laid. It is fairly slow to establish in the first few years but thereafter grows acceptably quickly. Its masses of spring blossom attract insects and the dense structure is hugely attractive to many nesting birds. An excellent wildlife hedge

Hedge	Special feature
Hazel (*Corylus avellana*)	Useful in mixed hedges but open-structured. It is scarcely practical to expect a neat hedge and a good crop of nuts (which of course are highly desirable for wildlife) but it is sensible and attractive to leave a small number of catkins when trimming
Holly (*Ilex aquifolium*)	Holly hedges are probably the most impenetrable of all; and so are attractive to birds for nesting although the dry prickly carpet of leaves that accumulates beneath will deter much other wildlife
Hornbeam (*Carpinus betulus*)	Superficially very similar to beech although not related to it, hornbeam is not as suitable for hedging because it does not retain its dead leaves as effectively through the winter
Laurel (*Prunus laurocerasus*)	One of the great evergreen hedging plants of the past, its drawback is the difficulty associated with pruning the enormous leaves. Of some merit for nesting birds
Lawson cypress (*Chamaecyparis lawsoniana*)	Fast growth and a dense screening effect have made Lawson cypress irresistible in modern gardens; and it is attractive for nesting birds. But, like all fast-growing plants, it requires constant attention to prevent it from becoming too tall
Leyland cypress (x *Cupressocyparis leylandii*)	This plant is best avoided. Although its rapid growth can be a virtue, this is offset in most gardens by its potentially enormous size that can lead to serious problems. It was the plant most targeted by recent legislation intended to limit 'nuisance hedges'
Lonicera	The shrubby relative of the honeysuckle called *Lonicera nitida* is a useful if rather unexciting plant for a dense, low hedge. It has some value for nesting birds but little additional wildlife merit
Privet (*Ligustrum*)	This rather dismal plant drains the soil of moisture and nutrients and so inhibits other vegetation. The native species *Ligustrum vulgare* (most hedging privet is the Japanese *Ligustrum ovalifolium*) has some value for its black fruits, which birds eat
Sea buckthorn [1] (*Hippophae rhamnoides*)	Thorny, deciduous shrub with narrow, silvery leaves. Grown as free-standing plants with male plants nearby for pollen, females produce many orange berries late in the year. It is a good windbreak hedge in coastal gardens but clipping limits berry production
Yew [2] (*Taxus baccata*)	A beautiful dense evergreen and overall, probably the finest garden hedge – but too dense for much wildlife. Moreover, almost all parts are poisonous to cattle and horses
Thuja plicata	The least well-known, least widely planted of the good hedging conifers. An excellent alternative to Lawson cypress

Boundary walls and fences

Boundary walls or fences usually exist when you purchase your property; which means your wildlife options are limited to making the most of them. But in new gardens, or in older gardens where the existing boundary is derelict, you may have the opportunity to make wildlife-friendly improvements.

While there is no better, more wildlife-friendly boundary for a garden than a hedge (*see p.98*), I realise there are many gardens where a hedge is impracticable – because it would be too expensive, would look inappropriate or, usually, because the owner simply requires a boundary more quickly than even the fastest-growing hedge can offer.

The other possibilities therefore are a wall or a fence but before considering their relative wildlife merits, it is important to consider what is expected of any boundary, whether a wall, fence or hedge. There is in practice often a legal requirement that is not generally appreciated: a requirement to fence (or less frequently to maintain a wall or hedge) to define the boundary. But in any event, a protective boundary is desirable if for instance you keep livestock in your garden (when you would be liable for any damage they cause when straying) or if you have some hazard such as a pool into which a neighbour might fall. But apart from any prudent or obligatory legal requirements, a sound boundary will afford you privacy and, most importantly, shelter.

Shelter from wind

The type of shelter from which you, your garden and your garden wildlife will benefit most is shelter from the wind. Protection from the wind benefits plants enormously. Although the wind is a potent physical force and can of course uproot or break large trees, this is relatively infrequent. Much more significant is that it is a highly potent drying force that stunts plant growth.

Right The many holes and passageways within traditional dry stone walls attract all kinds of wildlife.

You will see evidence of this most clearly on an exposed cliff or mountain where the trees and shrubs are all noticeably stunted – the wind dries moisture from the leaf surfaces faster than the plant is able to replace it from the soil and also causes the death of buds through literally drying them out. Most insects don't thrive in windy places because they don't have the strength to cope, and where there are fewer insects, there will be fewer of the many other creatures that feed on them.

The most efficient barrier for diminishing the wind strength should be 50 per cent permeable – in other words, one that is half holes. The research that revealed this also showed that the main benefits from the lessening of wind strength are apparent for a distance to leeward equal to about ten times its height – so a 2m high barrier will provide good protection for about 20m, adequate for most gardens. The choice then lies between the various types of walls and fences and it's here that wildlife considerations are important.

Dry stone walls

Most traditional walls are fairly solid structures, lacking the desirable 50 per cent permeability and therefore prone to induce eddies to form; but robust enough to withstand the full force of the wind. In many parts of

the country, dry stone or other types of wall have become integral parts of the landscape and should always be used in areas where they are a traditional feature – provided it is possible still to find craftsmen able to build them.

Dry stone walls are magnificent for wildlife because of the warren of tiny holes and passageways within. I realise they are havens for snails but they are havens for many other small creatures too. Some use them as temporary shelters for hibernation or nesting, for many others they are permanent homes. Countless species of insect, spider and other invertebrates, rodents like mice and voles, insectivores such as shrews, bats if the wall is big enough, amphibians (frogs, newts and toads will all use them) and reptiles (if you are especially lucky, you may have lizards in your wall) will benefit.

Many birds are attracted by dry stone walls, partly as perches, partly because of the food they find on, in and near them, but also as nesting sites – tits, robins, flycatchers and others will make nests in walls. Crevices and ledges will collect small particles of wind-blown soil and before long, mosses will colonise, to be followed by small ferns and flowering plants. The process can

sometimes be speeded up for interesting wall-loving plants by scattering a mixture of seeds and soil into gaps in the wall or by introducing one or two plants which should then flower and self-seed.

Many gardeners will understandably plead that they don't have the space, opportunity or resources to have a dry stone wall. I don't, but so valuable and interesting are they that I have very easily created a replica of a partly tumbled down wall in my own wildlife garden for the special habitat it offers (*see p.166*).

Brick walls

In many old town gardens, brick walls are important features of the urban landscape and whenever practicable should be repaired rather than replaced. But bricks can be expensive and in modern gardens, modern materials are appropriate and a large range

Below left Plants growing from a wall built from many thin pieces of slate.
Below An old limestone wall provides fertile ground for wildlife.

Above A ranch-style wind-permeable fence backed by a fuchsia hedge.

of attractive and relatively inexpensive building blocks is now available. By and large, brick or block-built walls don't have holes in them but this doesn't mean they have no wildlife value. The fact that they are solid, rigid structures makes them ideal habitats for lichens; and the rough surface of some modern replica bricks renders them especially so. There's a general and reasonably accurate belief that lichens are slow-growing. But patience will be rewarded. A fairly moist north-facing boundary wall to my garden that I see every day from my study window was built from old bricks 18 years ago. It has been colonised by the common orange lichen, *Xanthoria*, and the largest colony is now 1250mm in diameter; not huge but with perhaps 100 colonies in total on the wall, they certainly make a fine sight when they are caught in the glow of the morning sun.

Fencing

The most popular modern fence is built from panels of some form of horizontal overlapping softwood planks. But it is the most popular because it is the cheapest. It lacks both wind permeability and physical strength and where financial constraints dictate that this must be the choice, you should ensure that most vertical posts are braced by a diagonal.

I prefer to sink the vertical posts at least 60cm into the ground and to ram them in, rather than use concrete – they will thus be much simpler to replace in years to come. Don't be dragooned by a fencing contractor or salesman into accepting posts sunk only 45cm or worse, 30cm, simply because that is his standard practice.

The life of softwood panelled fences can be increased by using soil boards at the base to protect the main structure from contact with the ground. Much more

Above left Support each post with a
temporary brace while the concrete sets.
Above right Improve the look of a fence
by erecting trellis along the top.

robust, although considerably more costly than
horizontal soft boards are thicker, vertical wooden
boards in the pattern usually called feather boarding.
The somewhat drab effect of any wooden panel fence
can be relieved by having the posts 30cm taller than the
fence and erecting trellis along the top. This will enable
you to train roses, clematis or other climbers most
attractively but you should be aware that this will add
to the structural instability – especially if you use
evergreen climbers which will present a considerable
surface area to strong winter gales.

But there is one important wildlife advantage of
wooden panels – they offer a huge number of nooks,
crannies and ledges; perfect places for insects and
other small invertebrates to shelter, hibernate or breed.
Examine almost any wooden fence more than about

one year old and you will see a multitude of spiders'
nests, pupae of butterflies and moths and clusters of
hibernating insects such as ladybirds. The greatest
enemy of the wildlife that lives on and in your fence is
wood preservative and paint. I fully understand that
gardeners want to obtain the maximum life for their
fence and may indeed want it a particular colour. My
suggestion is to paint or treat it once, when it is first
erected. Use a long-life modern wood treatment product;
and then, if at all possible, resist doing it again.

Admittedly more costly than softwood panels is a
traditional rural alternative that has greater durability,

permeability and a much more attractive appearance. It is now possible to buy hurdles, usually of interwoven willow or hazel and constructed in various standard sizes. The price varies widely – those that are handmade by craftsmen are understandably the most expensive. Indeed, the more enterprising fencing manufacturers are producing ranges of durable rustic fencing in several different patterns that are well worth seeking out before you commit yourself to a major outlay. I am unsure if they have any special wildlife benefits over cheaper wooden fences by they look immeasurably better.

The ideal, for the gardener requiring instant shelter and privacy but with the vision to plan for the future of the garden, is to use fence panels of some kind but then to plant a hedge, preferably on the sunny side of them. By the time the hedge has matured, the panels can be removed – and if they happen to be interwoven hurdles, they will in any event be approaching the end of their lives.

Below Climbing plants can be trained along a woven hazel fence.

Containers

Growing plants artificially in tubs or pots is an ancient practice – remains of plant pots have been found at Pompeii and other important archaeological sites. They were probably popular then for much the same reasons as now – they are attractive in their own right and allow us to grow plants in places where there is no soil.

There's nothing natural about a plant container as we understand it in a gardening sense. You will sometimes find very small pockets of soil naturally confined in a hollow in rocks or on an old tree trunk and although they can be important habitats for mosses and other small plants (*see p.72*) and as such are worth mimicking in gardens, they aren't really equivalent to the type of container I have in mind here.

Adding slow-release fertiliser pellets

All potting composts contain a finite amount of nutrients so supplementary feeding with either an organic or an artificial fertiliser is essential. I can see no reason not to make life easy for yourself by using slow-release artificial fertiliser pellets in containers. This eliminates the need for the chore of weekly attention; although of course routine watering can't be avoided unless you install an automated watering system.

The big advantage of containers is that they offer an opportunity to grow plants just about anywhere. Placing containers close to the house, for example – closer than is generally feasible or practicable with beds and borders – can mean almost bringing the garden into your home. One of the pleasures I look forward to towards the end of summer every year is when the large tubs of species pelargoniums close to one of our windows prove so attractive to humming bird hawk moths.

But container gardening isn't simply about putting soil in a pot and planting something in it. By placing soil in a container you disturb its make-up – the pore and crumb structure is destroyed – and drainage is also impeded. As a result, the soil soon oscillates between being extremely dry and hard and being waterlogged.

For this reason, in a container you need an artificial compost, one that either contains no soil or in which the soil is augmented with organic matter to provide the correct balance between drainage and water retention. The most widely used soil-based compost for many years has been the John Innes range, developed at the John Innes Research Institute in the 1930s.

There is also now a multiplicity of soil-less composts, which are easier and lighter to handle. Many, however, are still based on peat, which shouldn't be used by any gardener today unless for some very specific purpose for which nothing else will work. Choose composts based on peat alternatives like composted paper, straw, sewage waste, coir fibre or other materials. And don't forget that the original John Innes formula requires the addition of peat to the soil – soil-based composts amended with peat alternatives are now available and preferable.

Weathered terracotta

....

Other than for plant-raising, plastic containers have little or no part to play in wildlife gardening. Since they are impermeable, the compost in them soon becomes waterlogged and anaerobic. Terracotta is a much better choice as it allows air to pass through, and your plants will be immeasurably healthier. Terracotta containers, especially those made of hand-thrown clay, are not only intrinsically more attractive, but they have rough outer surfaces that trap minute amounts of water together with organic matter and mineral dust particles. As a result they soon look appealingly weathered. Depending on how long they are left undisturbed, algae, mosses and lichens will then grow on them. The outer surface of an old container can be one of the most important microhabitats in the garden.

There is no reason why native plants can't be grown in containers but because of the generally short flowering period of herbaceous perennials and annuals, I find they are seldom satisfactory. It makes more sense

to confine short-term container planting to exotics – conventional hardy and half-hardy bedding plants and bulbs. These will attract plenty of pollinating insects and, if you choose carefully, can also be appealing to a few species of butterflies and moths.

Shrubs and small trees

A special advantage offered by large containers is that they allow you to grow shrubs and even small trees where otherwise this would be impossible. If the container is large enough and the tree or shrub appropriate, you might even find it possible to attract birds to nest – with or without the provision of an artificial nest box. Small conifers are most likely to be successful in this respect.

I have come to appreciate how useful a container-grown tree can be in another way, however, and this provides a perfect example of what I call the 'portable habitat' approach. I have a 20-year-old 'John Downie' crab apple in a large terracotta tub in a small courtyard close to the house. The tree is grafted on the dwarfing

apple rootstock M27 and so is only about 1.5m tall. It provides us with a beautiful display of blossom in the spring and we have the pleasure of seeing both the flowers and the insects the flowers attract. In due course it supplies a crop of sumptuous orange-red fruits which are ample for our annual crab apple jelly supply – 'John Downie' is much the best variety for making jelly. Excess fruit are appreciated by the birds but there is an additional virtue of this little tree in that it provides somewhere for me to hang a tubular bird seed feeder. I use sunflower seed in this feeder which is welcomed by a different range of birds from those that feed on the fruits. The birds drop the husks from the sunflower seeds onto the surface of the compost in the container to provide a moisture-retaining and most attractive much. Yet more birds, ground-feeding species like blackbirds and pigeons, then forage amongst the mulch for seeds and for the insects hiding beneath. All told, we have a multitude of kinds of wildlife close to the house and all made possible by the combination of a large container, a modern compost, a slow-release fertiliser and the ingenuity of the developer of the dwarfing rootstock.

Vegetables and fruit

Fruit and vegetables are a magnet for wildlife. The profusion of rich, succulent growth that is so appealing to us appeals equally to other creatures although in truth, most of them are pests. Having a wildlife and kitchen garden in close proximity therefore is about careful management to achieve a balance.

With vegetables, it's logical to start with soil preparation. I have always believed that the secret of keeping soil-inhabiting pests under control is to turn the plot over regularly with a fork in late winter. This brings slugs to the surface, along with soil-inhabiting insect larvae like cutworms, wireworms and chafer grubs as well as the pupae of numerous moths and flies.

Slugs and larvae will make their way down again but there is almost bound to be a robin nearby to catch some before they do and if the operation is repeated several times, other birds will be encouraged to come and scratch at the surface to reduce the population further. Not only does this operation offer excellent pest control but it is as valuable as anything in bringing birds into the garden or allotment at this time of year. There's no point, however, in trying to break up the soil in midwinter when the ground is hard. You can do more harm than good because heavy rain may beat a surface that is too finely broken into a hard cap.

Much as insect-eating birds are welcome in late winter, by sowing and planting time in spring, the balance has swung the other way and seed-eating birds or omnivorous species like blackbirds, which want to scratch the disturbed soil for whatever they can find, are less appreciated. Traditional scarecrows may have a part to play in large vegetable plots or allotments but I urge you to resist the temptation to use any and every bird-deterring device regardless of its appearance.

I have a particular antipathy to bits of coloured plastic fluttering in the breeze like a multitude of cheap flags on a public holiday. Of course no-one wants all their hard work undone by birds but if kitchen gardening is about anything, it's about aesthetics as well as productivity. In just the same way as the nation needs energy, it will be extremely sad if defacing the countryside with wind turbines proves to be the only solution.

For smaller vegetable plots, I find that lightweight fruit cage netting placed over seed beds until the seeds have emerged affords adequate protection. Support the netting on upturned plant pots placed atop bamboo canes. Never, ever, use black cotton or similar materials in which birds can easily become fatally entangled.

Sowing extra seeds

If you are prepared to run the risk of needing extra thinning, then simply sowing slightly more thickly than is ideal will help compensate you for any losses. Remember the old country adage about sowing that runs: 'One to rot and one to grow; One for pigeon, one for crow.' In truth, it is large seeds like beans and peas that are at the greatest risk from birds, pigeons especially, and whilst the protection for broad and dwarf beans must be removed as they emerge, with peas the netting can be permanent.

As soon as you have sown pea seeds, put the support netting in place. I realise that pea support net has a wide mesh, too wide physically to keep out birds, even big ones like wood pigeons, but it will still act as a effective deterrent. Traditional twiggy stick supports for peas work equally well but not many gardeners have ready access to these and certainly no-one should hack lumps off countryside hedges. In rural areas, it is worth making contact with a farmer who is planning hedge maintenance in autumn and winter to see if twigs might be available for you to collect. Runner beans can present a problem because the support canes must be in place when the seeds are sown and it isn't easy to put even temporary netting over them. I find that the best solution is to sow three seeds at each position and remove any spare seedlings if all survive and emerge. Some gardeners routinely transplant runner beans but

Above left Traditional scarecrows are effective bird scarers for larger plots.
Below left Twiggy sticks will support your peas and keep birds away.
Above A good support system for your runner beans is essential. Sow three seeds at each position and then remove any spare seedlings if all survive and emerge.

Right Apple blossom in spring.
Below The best way to protect vegetables like brassicas is to use cages or netting.

Leaving crops to flower

There are rather few positive aspects of vegetable growing for wildlife. If you have room, you might try leaving a few of the many biennial vegetable crops, like brassicas, parsnips, carrots and parsley, in place to flower the following season. They will be greatly appreciated by bees and other pollinating insects. The yellow flowers of brassicas (*above*) are especially attractive to insects.

I abandoned this many years ago because I find establishment from direct sowing is much better.

If mice and voles present a serious problem by removing pea and bean seeds, as they are very likely to do in rural areas, try laying fine-mesh chickenwire over the soil surface after the seeds have been sown (*see p.62*). It can stay in place throughout the life of the crop and be taken up and re-used the following year. There are no longer any approved deterrent chemicals for seed treatment and you should at all costs avoid using traps. You will kill an animal every time you lay a trap and may injure pets and birds, too.

Established vegetable crops are, of course, also at risk (*see p.195* for more about environmentally friendly methods of insect pest control) but birds pose a threat, too. Vegetable crops most at risk are brassicas – cabbages, cauliflowers, Brussels sprouts and so forth – which can be stripped wholesale by pigeons in hard winters. As with seeds, scarecrows have some merit but netting is the only really satisfactory option.

Prolonging blossoming and fruiting

With fruit trees, it is their massed blossom that is hugely beneficial. When apple, pear and plum trees are in flower in spring, they act like magnets for honey bees and other insect species. I have said that if apple trees would only bloom for longer than a week, you would hardly want for any other ornamental tree. If you have room, you can prolong both the ornamental appeal and the value to insects by having a selection of varieties that flower in sequence. The option of choosing apple varieties grafted on dwarfing rootstocks means that several trees can be fitted into a relatively small space.

Another option is to have a so-called family tree in which more than one variety is grafted on the same rootstock. A slight problem arises because the varieties for family trees are chosen for their compatibility – they will pollinate each other - and this means they must flower at more or less the same time. My solution to prolong the appeal both to us and pollinating insects – and ultimately to prolong the fruiting season – is to have a fruit tunnel and a row of cordons composed of varieties that flower and fruit in sequence. My apple tunnel occupies only 10m by 1.5m but gives us blossom over several weeks and then fruit over several months. The blossom flows like a wave from the earliest variety 'Irish Peach' at one end to the latest, 'Pitmaston Pineapple' at the other; and bees and other pollinating insects follow it.

When tree fruits mature and ripen, wildlife again takes a serious interest. In truth, most people scarcely notice wasps other than when plums are ripening, when individual insects are pursued with swatters or rolled-up newspapers. This doesn't matter much but when their nests are destroyed it is most unfortunate. For much of the year, wasps play an important part in the balance of life in the garden by catching insects and other creatures to feed to their young. Unlike bees which feed on nectar, wasps are carnivorous and only when nests are in houses or close to areas where children or people with allergies to the stings may come into contact with them should they be destroyed.

Although wasps are the most obvious creatures to be attracted to ripening fruit, their importance for birds shouldn't be overlooked. I have several large old apple trees and when the excess fruits drop, there is scarcely an apple on the ground that doesn't show some evidence of pecking and quite commonly, there is barely more than the skin remaining. If you have large trees and plenty of excess fruit, don't be too assiduous in collecting windfalls. If you have only a small number of fruit on small trees, you will want to pick regularly before the apples have time to drop.

Left The author's apple tunnel with a succession of varieties giving blossom and fruit over a long period.

Above A fruit cage is easy to construct and will protect your fruit at harvest time but still allow access by insects in spring.

Protecting soft fruit

With soft fruit, the problems and decisions are different. In many parts of the country, it is all but impossible to grow currants, raspberries, loganberries and other soft fruit without protection from birds. The fruits will be devoured by a large number of species while the buds will fall prey to others, especially finches. Although bullfinches are now much less common than formerly, they alone were once reason enough for having a fruit cage and I do believe that if you are serious in your wish to produce a crop, a cage is essential.

Proprietary cages with aluminium frames and lightweight netting can now be bought relatively inexpensively. It used to be said that netting prevented pollinating insects from entering and that they wouldn't fly through the holes even if physically small enough to do so. It was, and sometimes still is, suggested that the roof be rolled back at blossom time to facilitate them. I can only quote my own experience, which is that this is a complete fallacy. I have a robust cage made from wooden posts with fine-mesh chickenwire sides and a lightweight netting top. Insects have no problem entering and we always have superb crops.

Rock gardens

Also rather grandly called alpine beds, rock gardens aren't usually major contributors to the wildlife value of gardens. But there is one special feature that alpine plants offer – they flower particularly early in the season, providing emerging insects with much sought-after nectar when it might otherwise be in short supply.

An alpine challenge

One other way in which an alpine trough or small alpine bed can be put to interesting wildlife garden use is by devoting it to native British mountain plants, as I have done with a large old farm trough that I inherited. This could prove something of a challenge for several reasons: there isn't a huge variety of species, many are rare in the wild and consequently are not sold either as seed or plants by many nurseries, and many aren't readily compatible in the same container. This is because their needs reflect the wide range of mountain soil conditions that exist in the British Isles – some require highly acidic soil and some highly alkaline soil.

For me, however, it has proved a fascinating exercise and one I would encourage you to take up. The plants that have so far proved most successful are: alpine lady's mantle (*Alchemilla alpina*), alpine meadow rue (*Thalictrum alpinum*), alpine poa (*Poa alpina*), hoary rock-cress (*Draba incana*), mat grass (*Nardus stricta*), moss campion (*Silene acaulis*), mountain avens (*Dryas octopetala*), mountain saxifrage (*Saxifraga oppositifolia*) above, mountain violet (*Viola lutea*), mountain willowherb (*Epilobium montanum*), rock cinquefoil (*Potentilla rupestris*), and thrift (*Armeria maritima*).

To grow alpine plants successfully, it's essential to mimic as closely as possible the conditions of their natural habitat – which is almost certainly not the Alps although it is likely to be a mountainous region somewhere. In areas such as these, plants are subject to high rainfall, strong winds, free-draining soil with very little organic matter, and widely fluctuating temperatures. Remember that although a mountain top can be bitterly cold on a winter's night, it can experience searing heat at midday in summer.

The enemies of alpine plants at lower altitudes are clinging damp – either cold or warm. Both encourage rotting of flowers and leaves. For this reason, alpine plants in gardens are often surrounded by stone chips to avoid soil being splashed on to them and are sometimes grown in special greenhouses with no heat but plenty of ventilation. These conditions may also help discourage pests such as slugs, snails and insects but they also render the whole miniature habitat rather sterile.

To offer any benefit to wildlife, alpine plants need to be grown in the open in an alpine trough or other container rather than enclosed in an alpine greenhouse. It's a characteristic of most alpines that they flower early in the season, taking advantage of the short warm spring and summer after the snows have melted in order to produce their seeds before unfavourable conditions return in the autumn. If you see alpines in flower early in the year in their natural habitat, even those growing in really extreme conditions high on mountains or in the far north (or far south in the southern hemisphere), you will find them being visited by pollinating insects. These too telescope their life cycles into the same brief period

and offer fascinating examples of nature at its most adaptable. Alpines are all short, tufted plants with flowers close to soil level, tucked away from the strongest winds which would damage them and blow pollen away before it had any chance to do its job. The insects, too, must stay close to the ground so they don't fall victim to mountain winds and therefore are handily placed to offer the plants a pollination service.

This early flowering feature will also be appealing to garden insects because in most gardens, there are relatively few flowers, apart from bulbs, in the early part of the season so insects emerging prematurely may suffer severely from a food shortage. This is especially significant in abnormally cold springs when nectar-producing alpines can provide a highly valuable function. There is room for an alpine trough in the smallest of gardens; and cost is no bar because

attractive troughs made from replica stone are readily available. Choose a free-draining potting compost with a low nutrient content – a soil-based blend like John Innes No.3 mixed in the ratio of one part of compost to three parts of horticultural grit will work well with most common alpines.

Whilst the choicest species are both expensive and a challenge to grow, there are numerous kinds that do adapt fairly well to lowland garden conditions. I give my plants a light dressing with bone meal early in the year – anything containing much nitrogen will encourage soft, disease-prone foliage. I try to minimise problems arising from damp conditions by promptly picking off any dead leaves or flowers and by removing any leaves that blow in from elsewhere.

Easy alpines and bulbs

On the next two pages are my suggestions for a range of easy-to-grow alpines and bulbs that flower in profusion in late winter or early spring in most areas. They will be appreciated as nectar sources by early-season garden insects. I have simply listed plants that I know and that I know to be reliable but the best way, of course, to choose early flowering plants of any kind is to visit your local nursery or garden centre at the appropriate time of year and buy whatever is in bloom. (See *p.168–9* for information on native rock plants to grow on walls.)

Easy to grow alpines and bulbs/1

Alpine	Special features
Anemone apennina	Bright blue, star-like flowers
Anemone blanda [1]	Star-like flowers in blue, purple, pink or white
Anemone blanda 'White Splendour'	Large white flowers
Anemone nemorosa (wood anemone) [2]	White, cup-shaped flowers often flushed with pink
Anemone nemorosa 'Robinsoniana'	Pale lavender-blue flowers with grey reverses
Cyclamen coum [3]	A very variable cyclamen; the leaves may be plain or patterned with either grey or silver and the flowers may be pink, red or white
Cyclamen coum pallidum 'Album'	Purple blotches at the base of the petals
Cyclamen coum 'Roseum'	Rich rose-pink flowers
Eranthis hyemalis (winter aconite) [4]	Bright, shiny, yellow flowers above a ruff of bright green leaves
Hacquetia epipactis	Yellow flowers next to green bracts usually appear before the leaves
Hepatica nobilis (liverleaf)	Bowl-shaped flowers in blue, pink or white
Iberis semperflorens	A spreading mat of scented white flowers
Cushion saxifrages (Kabschia or Porophyllum saxifrages)	A wonderful group of mostly early-flowering, slow-growing alpines. The rosettes or leafy shoots often have lime encrustations. There are numerous varieties and only a few flower in mid- to late spring. If you visit an alpine nursery in late winter, most of the saxifrages in flower will be of this type

Easy to grow alpines and bulbs/2

Bulb	Special features
Crocus angustifolius	Orange-yellow flowers marked with bronze
Crocus chrysanthus 'Blue Pearl' **[5]**	Blue flowers with yellow throats
Crocus chrysanthus 'Ladykiller'	Cream flowers with yellow throats
Crocus chrysanthus 'Zwanenburg Bronze'	Slender flowers in shades of silvery lavender to reddish-purple
Crocus tommasinianus	White, cup-shaped flowers often flushed with pink
Crocus tommasinianus 'Whitewell Purple'	Reddish-purple flowers with silvery mauve insides
Galanthus nivalis (common snowdrop) **[6]**	Many varieties but 'Atkinsii' is notable for its size and earliness
Iris 'Cantab'	Pale blue flowers with yellow markings
Iris 'Harmony'	Royal blue flowers with yellow markings
Iris 'J S Dijt'	Reddish-purple flowers with orange markings
Iris 'Katharine Hodgkin'	Pale blue flowers marked with yellow and blue veins
Iris reticulata	Fragrant flowers in various shades of blue, violet or purple, all with central yellow markings
Muscari armeniacum **[7]**	Purple-blue flowers; can be invasive
Muscari latifolium	Pale blue flowers at top of the spike; violet-blue flowers at base
Scilla sibirica 'Spring Beauty' **[8]**	Electric blue, delicate, nodding flowers
Tulipa biflora	Star-like white flowers with red margins and yellow centres
Tulipa clusiana var. *chrysantha*	Bowl-shaped yellow flowers with red or brown outsides
Tulipa kaufmanniana	Bowl-shaped flowers in cream, yellow, pink, orange or red
Tulipa linifolia 'Bronze Charm'	Orange-bronze flowers

Trees

The description of a tree as a microcosm of the world is a slight exaggeration perhaps, but the essence of the comment is accurate enough. A microcosm of a wood might be closer to the mark because it's unarguable that other plants, as well as many animals, depend on individual trees for their own survival.

Any tree in your garden will have a bearing on your garden as a wildlife habitat. And as many gardeners choose perhaps only two or three trees in a gardening lifetime, it's a choice that needs to be made wisely. Many people moreover acquire one or more mature trees with their gardens and their size alone renders them pivotal features.

Apart from their sheer physical presence and the fact that they dominate visually, why do trees have such an influence on their surroundings? First, their leaf and root volume means they extract huge volumes of water from the soil – it has been calculated that 1sq m of leaf area loses 5 litres of water per day in the summer and so the volumes lost from a large tree may only be guessed at. Second, they extract a large amount of nutrients from the soil. The two features mean that other plants nearby must either adapt or starve. Plants that live naturally or are related to those that live naturally in woodland therefore are most likely to thrive under a garden tree.

Trees also cast shade, so only plants and creatures that can tolerate low light levels will successfully live beneath them – although there is a significant difference between deciduous and evergreen trees here. Deciduous species, especially those like oaks that come into leaf fairly late in the spring, can permit a considerable range of plants to grow and flower beneath them in the early part of the year – think of the carpets of bluebells in oak woods in spring. Conifers cast a perpetual, fairly dense shade and if the darkness is truly great, as it is beneath yews, little will survive. I have described gardening beneath a large yew tree as like gardening at night.

Finally, and most unappreciated, is the fact that trees harbour other forms of life, which can work for or against your wildlife gardening objectives. Oaks are good examples with which to start because more creatures are dependent on or make use of our two native oak species, the sessile oak (*Quercus petraea*) and the pedunculate oak (*Quercus robur*) than any other kind of tree in Britain. There are many hundreds of species of moth, beetle and other insect (more than 40 are

Sycamore – alien invader

There are those trees that are common and widely grown but with little or no wildlife value. Unsurprisingly, they aren't native species but aliens that have been parachuted in amongst our indigenous wildlife to no beneficial effect. The ultimate is the sycamore (*Acer pseudoplatanus*). It arrived in Britain in the late 16th century, and almost certainly has fewer other organisms associated with it than any other British tree. Apart from the fungi that cause tar spot and sooty bark diseases, several species of aphid and sooty mould and the North American grey squirrel (*Sciurus carolinensis*), it's hard to think of anything that would suffer significantly by its absence. Sycamores have no place or value in gardens, and if they do have any wildlife merit, it is far beyond our gardens – they have some value as one of the few kinds of tree that will grow on and help to stabilise sand dunes. A rough rule of thumb is that the more recently a naturalised tree was introduced to this country, the less value it is likely to have for wildlife.

responsible for causing conspicuous galls), many kinds of spider and other invertebrates. Over 400 lichen species have been found growing on oaks, along with around 65 kinds of moss and liverwort and over 4,000 different fungi. Many birds and several mammals are also frequently associated with oak trees. Should we all have oaks in our gardens therefore to be sure of doing our bit to maintain biodiversity? Patently not, because

oaks grow large and unless our gardens are also very large, our 'normal' gardening activities will suffer. If you already have a garden oak tree, then be pleased, be grateful and adapt your plantings accordingly – try visiting an oak wood to obtain some initial ideas.

Fastigiate trees

If you don't have an oak but would like to make a gesture towards its importance, or grow another attractive, wildlife-valuable native tree, then investigate the option of growing a fastigiate form. Fastigiate trees are naturally occurring variants in which the branches grow vertically upwards, producing slender trees that laterally take up very little room; although some will nonetheless grow quite tall. A considerable number of fastigiate varieties exist, many of them of non-native species, generally with names like 'Fastigiata', 'Erecta', 'Columnaris' and 'Stricta'. The table below lists fastigiate forms of native trees although you may need to search for some in specialist nurseries.

Right *Carpinus betulus* 'Fastigiata' in the author's garden.

Fastigiate forms of native British trees

Species and cultivar	Common name	Species and cultivar	Common name
Aesculus hippocastanum 'Pyramidalis'	Horse chestnut	*Pinus sylvestris* Fastigiata Group	Scots pine
Betula pendula 'Fastigiata'	Silver birch	*Quercus robur* f. *fastigiata*	Oak
Carpinus betulus 'Columnaris'	Hornbeam	*Quercus robur* 'Hungaria'	Oak
Carpinus betulus 'Fastigiata'	Hornbeam	*Sambucus nigra* 'Pyramidalis'	Elder
Crataegus monogyna 'Stricta'	Hawthorn	*Sorbus aucuparia* 'Fastigiata'	Rowan
Fagus sylvatica 'Cockleshell'	Beech	*Taxus baccata* 'Fastigiata'	Yew
Fagus sylvatica 'Dawyck'	Beech	*Taxus baccata* 'Standishii'	Yew
Ilex aquifolium 'Green Pillar'	Holly	*Tilia cordata* 'Swedish Upright'	Small-leaved lime
Laburnum anagyroides 'Erect'	Laburnum	*Tilia platyphyllos* 'Fastigiata'	Large-leaved lime

Ornamental species

For gardeners who don't want a native tree, there is a multitude of exotic ornamental species that even in their normal, non-fastigiate form are small enough for many gardens. Much of what I have said about the wildlife value of ornamental shrubs is relevant here, and my advice is especially to avoid species with fully double flowers that offer no nectar, no pollen and no fruits. In reality, there is a fairly limited range of trees, or at least of tree genera, that have ornamental fruits and are suitable for small to medium-sized gardens. *Sorbus*, the genus that contains the mountain ash is perhaps the most important and most kinds are suitable, including the native mountain ash (*Sorbus aucuparia*) together with *Sorbus commixta*, *Sorbus* 'Joseph Rock' and *Sorbus vilmorinii* among others.

Next in importance are ornamental crab apples, which have the advantage of being available on the dwarfing rootstocks developed for apples. Among these I especially recommend *Malus floribunda*, *Malus* 'John Downie', *Malus* x zumi 'Golden Hornet', *Malus* x *moerlandsii* 'Profusion', and *Malus* 'Wisley Crab'. The two native hawthorns *Crataegus oxyacanthoides* and *Crataegus monogyna* are also excellent but do obtain the true species and for wildlife value don't be seduced into buying one of the many double-flowered forms which are undeniably attractive but yield no fruit.

All female hollies are good although rather slow-growing (males with no fruit are patently useless) but probably the best and most prolific producer of fruits is *Ilex aquifolium* 'J. C. van Tol'. Among other groups, there are several ornamental fruiting plums. including the wild cherry or gean (*Prunus avium*), sour cherry (*Prunus cerasus*) and bird cherry (*Prunus padus*), and the true form of honey locust (*Gleditsia triacanthos*) – not the commonly seen golden-foliaged variety 'Sunburst'. Most ornamental conifers have little or no food value for birds and although pines have some appeal for species that are equipped to remove the seeds, most don't produce cones until they are large and mature. Cypresses, which constitute the majority of garden conifers, are almost useless as food for birds or other garden creatures (apart from aphids) but they do have value as nesting sites. Many birds make use of their dense cover and I can almost guarantee that all the larger cypresses in my own garden will contain at least one nest every year; some have many. Trees of all kinds should also be used to support bird nesting boxes (*see p.56*). Whilst small nest boxes may be attached to all manner of supports, big boxes to appeal to big birds such as owls must be fixed high in large trees.

Right The wayfaring tree (*Viburnum lantana*) produces clusters of fragrant white flowers followed by red berries in autumn that later turn black.

Shrubs

Grouping two, three or four shrubs together is of far more benefit to wildlife than separating them around the garden. The closer your shrubbery is to emulating a woodland edge habitat, the more appealing it will be to birds, butterflies and other creatures that enjoy its shelter, dappled light and partial shade.

There's no formal division between shrubs and trees although I tend to use the name shrub for a plant that naturally (that is without pruning) won't exceed about 6m in height on a single stem. By this token, holly and bay are trees whereas *Philadelphus* is a shrub. However, some trees, like holly, are so slow-growing that they seldom reach real tree size in most gardens so I shan't be too strict in my interpretation here.

Few modern gardens are big enough to have a significant area devoted to shrubs in the manner so popular with gardeners of the past. But conversely, not many gardens are so small that there isn't room for at least few and whilst shrubs have an important part to play in mixed borders (*see p.84*), I do hope more gardeners will also consider grouping them.

Given the better security that is offered by a group planting, birds will be more likely to nest within the shrubs or to use artificial boxes put there for the purpose. An exposed nest box stuck on the side of an isolated shrub isn't likely to endear itself to other than the boldest bird. I also find positions close to shrubberies excellent places to site bird tables as they

Left Chaenomeles is a valuable early flowering shrub that later produces a valuable crop of fruits.
Right The rowan is a deciduous tree that produces scented blossom in spring, attracting many insects, and trusses of orange fruit in late summer.

afford the security of offering the birds somewhere to fly if danger threatens (*see p.52*). As with other plantings to encourage wildlife, you should select a mixture of native and exotic species and include both deciduous and evergreen types to provide shelter and cover at all times.

My view is that whilst shrubs with showy flowers are valuable for their overall aesthetic appeal, they have a less important part to play in attracting insects in the summer when perennials can fulfil that role. Early flowering shrubs are more valuable and those that produce a good crop of fruits later in the season especially so.

Fruiting shrubs

I can't over-emphasise the value of fruiting shrubs in the wildlife garden – you will often see them described as berrying shrubs although strictly, rather few of them produce berries in the botanical sense. You need only see the squabbling flocks of starlings (though sadly they aren't as common as once they were) and blackbirds feasting on them in the winter to appreciate their importance as a food source. And you may well find

Good yellow and white fruited shrubs and small trees

Shrub	Fruit colour	Notes
Cotoneaster salicifolius 'Rothschildianus'	Pale yellow	'Exburyensis' is similar; excellent trained as a standard
Euonymus myrianthus	Yellow	Fruits split to reveal orange seeds
Gaultheria mucronata 'Wintertime'	White	Needs acidic soil
Ilex aquifolium 'Bacciflava'	Mid-yellow	The best yellow-fruited holly
Malus 'Golden Hornet'	Mid-yellow	A crab apple; buy a plant grafted on the dwarfing rootstock M27
Pyracantha 'Soleil d'Or'	Deep yellow	Pyracanthas don't have to be trained against walls in the usual way; they make good free-standing shrubs
Skimmia japonica 'Kew White'	White	Evergreen, low-growing
Viburnum sargentii f. *flavum*	Pale yellow	The normal species has red fruits

Single-flowered roses to attract pollinating insects

Species/Variety	Type	Flower colour	Habit
'Canary Bird'	Hybrid of two Chinese species	Bright yellow	Upright, loose shrub
'Complicata'	Gallica	Mid-pink with paler centres	Tall shrub or short climber
'Dainty Bess'	Hybrid tea	Rose-pink	Small, upright bush
'Dunwich Rose'	Pimpinellifolia	Creamy white	Spreading shrub
'Fru Dagmar Hastrup'	Rugosa	Pale silver-pink	Small spreading shrub
Rosa bracteata 'Mermaid'	Hybrid from a Chinese species	Pale yellow	Tall climber
Rosa eglanteria 'Sweet Brier'	Native species	Soft pink	Tall, lax shrub
Rosa moyesii 'Geranium'	Near-species	Deep salmon-pink	Tall, spreading shrub
Rosa primula [right]	Central Asian species	Soft, pale yellow.	Spreading shrub
'White Wings'	Hybrid tea	White with brown stamens	Small upright bush

Above The waxwing is a winter visitor to Britain, where it feeds on berry-bearing shrubs and roses.
Right Double-flowered roses are of little value to bees and other pollinating insects because they rarely produce pollen.

fruiting shrubs offer almost the only attraction for some bird species that are otherwise seldom seen in gardens, like mistle thrushes, fieldfares and redwings. If you are lucky and live in the right areas, such exotics as waxwings may turn up, too. But yet again, the selection of fruiting shrubs must be a compromise. For most gardeners, the attractiveness of the fruits is the principal appeal so if birds take them all, there will be nothing left for us to enjoy. I find, however, that birds of most species tend preferentially to select red fruits and that in all except the coldest winters, other colours may be untouched. Just as with ornamental fruiting trees therefore (*see table, p.133*) yellow or white fruited shrub among the red will help ensure that at least some are left for us to appreciate.

Roses

I must say something about the relationship between roses and wildlife because despite some waning in their overall popularity, roses as a group are without

doubt the most widely grown of flowering shrubs and almost every garden has at least one. But whilst all roses are shrubs, they comprise a uniquely special category, their varied parentage reflected in a wide range of sizes and shapes, from tall, spreading shrubs, especially among some of the older varieties, to small, neat bushes among modern hybrid teas and floribundas, each with its own particular pruning regime. And of course, many are amenable to be trained and pruned, at one extreme as climbers or pillar plants and at the other as standards and half-standards. They also exhibit a wide range of flower sizes and forms, ranging from single through semi-double to fully double, all exhibiting a variety of colours and relative fragrance.

Just as with all other garden flowers, single-flowered roses are the most valuable kinds for wildlife as they produce both pollen and nectar. I shan't make myself popular with rose enthusiasts by saying that in general, the more modern, popular, floriferous and easy to grow the variety, the less it will achieve for wildlife. Most modern roses have double or semi-double flowers and whilst many have some fragrance and some nectar,

stamens and pollen are hard to find. You won't find many bees or other pollinating insects taking much interest in a bed of modern roses. They may fly in, attracted by the nectar, but they won't stay long because the dense, closely packed petals of the tight flowerheads are almost impossible to penetrate. By all means grow a few of the beautiful double-flowered modern or old roses in your garden – as I do – but mix with them a proportion of semi-double and most importantly, single-flowered kinds (*see box, above*).

Lawns

Even the average garden lawn is an important and under-appreciated habitat. It is especially important for invertebrates – and is likely to become more so now that gardeners aren't permitted to drench their turf with insecticides - although most of the creatures will pass unnoticed and unremarked.

There is a commonly held view that a lawn can only contribute to wildlife gardening when it is left unmown and so allowed to form the basis of a wild flower meadow. The notion, however, is wrong in almost every particular. First because an unmown lawn won't generally work as the foundation of a wild flower meadow because it comprises inappropriate types of grass. Moreover, it can in practice form the basis of a most fascinating habitat – a so-called waxcap lawn, which is one of the most striking, unusual and rewarding of all possible garden habitats for a gardener with patience. On a waxcap lawn you can expect to see

Left and below A short-cropped lawn is ideal for blackbirds to forage for worms.

some beautiful and rare species of toadstool provided no fertiliser, weedkiller or other chemicals are applied to it; although admittedly, the effects aren't swift to materialise (*see p.77*).

Even a normal lawn, fertilised and treated, can be expected to produce perhaps ten different species of toadstool, albeit rather small, brown and relatively unexciting kinds. And most gardeners almost certainly do want their lawns to remain 'normal' with attractive, closely mown grass, as green and lush as practicality and resources allow. A wild flower meadow is something quite different that they might want to create if they have space (*see p.156*).

Teeming with life

There will almost inevitably be some moss on an average garden lawn, possibly a small amount of lichen growth and a selection of lawn weeds, even when weed killers have been used. In moderation, all should be tolerated and some lawn weeds, especially lawn daisy (*Bellis perennis*) and blue-flowered slender speedwell (*Veronica filiformis*) can be particularly attractive.

Although there haven't been many detailed studies, one investigation found as many as 12 species of woodlice living on lawns and there are numerous insects, spiders and other creatures both above and below the soil surface. Some subterranean insect larvae, like wireworms and leatherjackets, may not be beneficial to the appearance of the lawn but they are the exceptions and lawns harbour few serious pests.

Research has revealed that lawn invertebrates fall into one of two categories - very small, fast-moving creatures that live near the tops of the grass blades and avoid danger by rapid escape, and organisms that live in the mulch layer of the soil where they avoid the lawn mower, and where the cushioning effect of the thatch of moss and dead grass minimises death due to trampling.

In many respects, they are similar to the creatures that live in grazed grassland although lawns are cut closer than grass is grazed. This is a reminder that over-assiduous removal of lawn thatch is to be avoided.

The role of earthworms

Worms are hugely important in providing aeration and drainage and maintaining soil fertility. In the past, chemicals were sold to repel or kill lawn worms but this was always the height of folly and is now illegal.

Only two of the 25 or so British species of earthworm produce casts, which are the mineral particles expelled after the organic bits of the soil have been digested. Other species of earthworm deposit the expelled matter in the upper parts of their burrows. The two cast-forming species are unusual in undergoing an aestivation – the summer equivalent of hibernation – and so their casts are found almost exclusively between October and May when they are active. The worms themselves are sometimes chanced upon coiled up in small, deep chambers if anyone happens to undertake deep digging in the summer.

A fertile garden of average size may contain 400,000 earthworms and cast densities of over 200 per sq m of lawn. Weights of 1kg of cast soil per square metre aren't exactly rare. Whilst lawn casts can be a nuisance in making the lawn slippery when it's wet and possibly creating small patches where weeds can become established, they disappear in the summer and I believe they simply have to be tolerated.

Raking or light scarifying once a year is certainly advantageous to the growth of the grass but to do more is unnecessary and harmful to the lawn's inhabitants.

You can certainly fertilise your lawn and apply weedkiller if you feel it necessary. But just don't overdo it. I have been appalled to discover one national lawn care company recommends four visits per year to include 'three granular feeds, one liquid feed, one moss control and three weedkillers' in spring, early summer, late summer and autumn/winter. That is seriously over the top and will certainly do nothing to enhance your lawn as a place for wildlife.

But perhaps the least appreciated value of a lawn is as an indicator - it is a silent witness to what happens in your garden when you aren't there -

especially at night. Slime trails reveal the activity of slugs and snails, small elongated droppings are testimony to the presence of hedgehogs, small holes are evidence that squirrels have been unearthing the nuts they buried in the autumn and of course, a fall of snow betrays where your cat went in the night and also the remarkable evidence of the large numbers of birds, mice, voles and other creatures that have passed by.

A garden lawn and a simple guide book to tracks, trails and signs are your windows to an extraordinary unseen wildlife world.

Below: Lawn daisies make tall, handsome plants when the lawn is not mown.
Right A mown path meanders through a wilder area where grass has been left to grow.

Hard landscaping

The modern term for paths, drives, paved areas, courtyards and patios, hard landscaping refers to parts of the garden that are essentially free of plants – other than those in containers. While these areas might seem to offer little potential for wildlife, in fact they have an important part to play in encouraging it.

The value and richness of the hard landscape habitat depends on the material from which it is made and most importantly, how many cracks it has – the more the better. Bricks or their modern equivalent, brick pavers, are best, followed by slabs of real or artificial stone, the smaller the better. Worst is anything uniform and visually monotonous such as concrete or tarmac.

In one sense, gravel ought to make an ideal habitat because it has more cracks and crevices than any other material. The evidence for this is apparent in the fact that unless a permeable membrane is laid underneath, weeds will appear in it anywhere. In practice, gravel isn't ideal because it has one other characteristic that makes it perfect for filling irregular spaces but works against it for most wildlife. It is unstable; it moves.

In my descriptions of the best places for mosses, lichens, fungi and many kinds of insect and other invertebrate to grow and thrive I have stressed the need for them to be undisturbed. That is what cracks in paving are and gravel isn't. Even in small inner-city gardens therefore where a lawn is undesirable or impractical, don't rely entirely on gravel or stone chips. Have at least a few areas of paving slabs – preferably with open joints and no mortar between them.

Rough surfaces

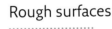

After the number of cracks and crevices, the most important feature of a hard landscaping material is its surface. Generally, the rougher it is, the better because an uneven surface will trap tiny soil particles and so give algae and mosses an opportunity to gain a foothold, to be followed in due course by other plant and small animal life. If you must use concrete, therefore, at least try to ensure it is brushed before it sets. Tarmac is apparently smooth but does have masses of small holes in the surface that will in time become colonised by mosses and other tiny plants. This does take a very long

Left: Thyme planted between pavers in the author's garden has spread to produce a carpet that is attractive to insects.

time, however, because the toxic chemicals in the tar must first be washed away although ultimately, areas of tarmac that aren't regularly walked on or driven over can build up considerable moss growth. Nonetheless, it receives my vote as the least valuable and appealing of all hard landscaping materials in gardens.

Hard landscaped areas are ideal places to site bird tables (on free-standing posts) and supports for bird feeders, not least because they are often close to the house where the birds can be observed. There is another advantage in having bird feeders on hard surfaces rather than soil in that the inevitable spillages of seed won't germinate and grow among other plants. They can simply be swept up.

By using containers, you can have whatever plants you choose on hard areas and the possibility of watching butterflies and other pollinating insects at close quarters even if you have no beds of open soil is rich return for a little time and effort in planting, feeding and watering.

Below Uneven surfaces and paving slabs with open joints have greater wildlife value than expanses of tarmac or concrete.

Cleaning landscaped areas

Almost the only living things that will grow on a completely smooth surface are microscopic algae. En masse, they will appear as a green film, not especially attractive to look at and making the surface extremely slippery when wet. Of course, no-one can be expected to tolerate a slippery, dangerous path but I would ask you, if at all possible, to avoid using chemical cleaning agents that will effectively sterilise any nooks and crannies and may run off into adjacent soil beds.

It's much better to use a jet washer (*above*) if you have access to one, or at the very least, to confine any chemical path cleanser only to the parts where it really is necessary.

Water gardens

The appeal of water is widely recognised and the water garden area is always one of the most popular at many garden centres. But water is valuable not only for its aesthetic value; it is hugely important for wildlife. It provides a habitat for aquatic creatures and attracts many more insects and animals in search of food and drink.

The type of pond most people want or already have – something fairly small and ornamental – is very different from a dedicated wildlife water garden, which is featured later in this book (*see p.180*). Here, I consider the ways in which a 'normal' water feature can be made wildlife-friendly and beneficial.

If you are starting from scratch, you have three decisions to make – where to site your pond, how big it should be and which material to use as lining. The siting of a pond is critical. The position should have as close as possible to eight hours of direct sunlight each day. This needn't apply to the whole surface area of the pond – half or even a third of the surface with full exposure to the sky is adequate, provided there is some water movement.

Size is also important. Self-contained water features will fit into the smallest of spaces and truly tiny pools can be constructed but the larger the pool, the easier it is to maintain a viable balance between water, plants and animal life. My experience is that the minimum effective size for an outdoor garden pool is about 1.5m by 1.2m with a depth of at least 30cm although so-called tub gardens are much smaller.

If possible, have shelving at the sides on which to stand baskets planted with aquatic plants. If you have inherited a pond from a previous owner and it has no shelving, all is not lost as plants, including water lilies, may be grown in baskets or pots submerged within the pond itself, elevated on bricks if necessary.

The choice of lining is a matter of expediency and cost. From a wildlife standpoint, there is little to choose for an ornamental pond between a rigid pre-formed liner, which gives you a strict and unalterable shape and depth, and butyl rubber sheeting. Depth is a variable option with both but should never be less than 45cm at the deepest part.

Providing water movement

In an essentially ornamental, relatively formal garden pond, you must have some water movement. A fountain will look attractive, will oxygenate the water and keep it ice-free for birds to drink in all except the coldest winters. This is provided simply and safely with a modern low-voltage pump kit, the low-voltage cable leading discreetly back to the nearest indoor power point. I can see no merit in using mains voltage, which must be installed by a electrical contractor and will be no more powerful or effective.

If you want a spectacular effect with a complex or extensive pattern of spray, have it by all means, but bear in mind that you won't be able to grow water lilies or other water plants successfully because most are intolerant of constant rain. You may also find that your ornamental fish won't thrive because the water will be over-oxygenated.

Above right A formal pond can be made more wildlife-friendly with extensive planting at the margins and a greater variety of water plants.
Below right A large, informal pool is more likely to be an attractive breeding site for insects such as dragonflies.

A modest fountain with a modest spray pattern will be good for your plants, good for your goldfish and good also in that other aquatic creatures may make use of the plants on which to live and breed. Try adding some submerged oxygenating plants too – not for their oxygenating value, which will be insignificant compared with your fountain, but to provide places in and among which small animals may live and breed. If you do have fish in your pond, you may find toads, frogs and newts will take no interest in it, or at best, will lay their spawn only for the tadpoles to be eaten. That said, I do think it's possible to strike a balance and my formal lily pond was for many years home both to a small number of goldfish and to breeding frogs and newts. It is imperative to provide amphibians with an escape route from ponds. If there are no marginal plantings to offer a way out, a ramp or other device must be provided.

Most ornamental pond plants are derived from exotic species and/or, like water lilies are complex hybrids. Nonetheless, rather few have double flowers and many therefore will attract at least some pollinating insects. And if they attract pollinating insects, you will stand a chance of seeing dragonflies that come to hunt them. It's fairly unlikely though that dragonflies will breed in a small pond with few marginal plants and without a substantial population of submerged creatures on which the dragonfly larvae will feed during their several years of submerged life. The benefit of a purpose-designed wildlife pond is nowhere more apparent than here; over ten years when my only garden pond was a small formal water-lily pond, I recorded five species of dragonfly in the garden. In the first five years after I constructed my dedicated wildlife pond, I noted 15.

Other 'water' features

There are many other features of garden wildlife to instruct and fascinate. The existing pond needn't be uprooted but can easily and quickly be converted into a bog garden. But valuable a habitat as a bog garden is, it lacks the sound and movement of water and the appeal that water has for wildlife. The answer lies with 'water features'. These include wall fountains in which water spills either from an amorphous spout or something like the mouth of an imitation classical mask.

Perhaps the simplest, most versatile features for wildlife are bubble or pebble fountains – small ground features such as piles of pebbles or single pieces of rock out of which, or over which, water trickles. They can be constructed piecemeal but purpose-made kits are now widely available. These comprise in effect a tiny plastic pond, complete with pump, that is placed in a hole in the ground and filled with rocks, pebbles or whatever takes your fancy. They remain ice-free during winter and whilst they won't harbour many living creatures, birds find them irresistible.

Cleaning and safety

Should garden ponds be cleaned out each year – or ever? Expert advice directed at making the pond attractive to amphibians suggests it should and I assume this is because a gradual build-up of leaves and other debris in the bottom may slowly foul the water and render it less attractive. But against that must be set the unavoidable disturbance and eradication of the many other creatures that live in pond mud and debris.

My own practice is to clear out my small formal pond every two or three years, carefully removing all fish and the plants (which are in pots or baskets) and then using a pond vacuum cleaner. My dedicated wildlife pond by contrast, is never cleared out (see p.182).

There is one most important aspect to water gardening that simply can't be avoided. Garden ponds and young children simply don't mix. It is wholly unrealistic to expect any parent to watch their infants continuously just as it is aesthetically unsatisfactory to have a garden pond and yet keep it permanently netted. An existing formal pond in a garden where young children live that can't be sensibly and attractively fenced should be filled in until they are older.

Right Damp-loving plants flourish along the banks of a stream and some will grow happily in a garden.
Below Where there is water, frogs and other amphibians are likely to be nearby.

ESTABLISHING A DEDICATED WILDLIFE GARDEN

There are almost as many ways to create and manage a wildlife garden as there are gardeners, so in this section of the book I explain the approach I have taken. It worked well for me and can serve as a template for anyone with comparable space and inclinations. If you have more or less space available than I do, you can scale up or down accordingly because all the same general principles apply. And whilst I can't promise that everything I have done and everything I have grown will necessarily work for you, at least I know it is successful sometimes!

Increasingly, gardeners are wanting to go further than simply garden in a wildlife-friendly, environmentally friendly way. More and more people are interested in setting aside and managing a part of their garden, or even the entire plot, solely for wildlife. In practice, there is no hard and fast line between the two approaches and a gardener who grows vegetables but is perfectly happy if the local fauna eat most of them clearly has a foot in both conventional and wildlife garden camps.

I have adopted two general principles in my own garden. First, because my wildlife garden is part of a much larger garden that is also managed in an environmentally friendly way and, like all gardens, contains many exotic species and conventional garden varieties, I felt justified in confining the wildlife area to native or naturalised plants. I like native plants, I don't grow them anywhere else in the garden and on balance I do believe they offer the best wildlife value (*see pp.89* for more about the relative wildlife merits of native and exotic species).

And second, I do want my wildlife garden to look attractive; as attractive as a tiny bit of wild countryside. For this reason, there aren't neglected vegetables to appeal to large white butterflies and rabbits, fruitless fruit bushes to keep the local finches happy or large areas taken over with rampant perennials like butterbur or coltsfoot just because the odd species of insect happens to feed on them. At the end of the day, this is a book about gardening, not wilderness management.

A word about allotments

Before I describe the preparation of a dedicated wildlife garden in detail, however, I would like to touch on a subject about which I feel strongly but which seems to thwart many well-intentioned potential wildlife gardeners. It should never be forgotten that there is an 'alternative' garden for many people in Britain; it is the allotment. Allotments date back to the late 19th century and their provision is regulated by law. If requested, a local authority must determine if there is sufficient demand for allotments and if so, they must provide them. There are stipulations about the types of building that may or may not be erected but little comment on the permitted horticultural activity.

However, for reasons that may be understandable, or may have been understandable in the past, local authorities amplify the legal conditions with by-laws and regulations that generally require a measure of tidiness. It is this legal trap that seems to have prevented a number of gardeners from turning their allotments into dedicated wildlife plots - for 'native plant garden' read 'neglected weedy plot'. I can see the point of view - people trying to produce vegetables and flowers may not take too kindly to such activities taking place next door.

My plea is for allotment holders themselves and local authorities to take a fresh look. As I stress many times in this book, a properly managed wildlife, native plant garden isn't a garden of weeds - although countless unoccupied allotments are!

Right Regulations requiring allotments to be kept tidy often deter would-be wildlife gardeners from growing native plants.

Doing the groundwork

The best way to create an easy-to-manage wildlife garden is to clear the area, even if the site contains native plants you would like to keep. On fertile ground, such as an old vegetable plot, you may need to remove nutrients from the soil. You will also need to use a rotavator to prepare the soil for sowing or planting.

So just how large must, or how small can, a dedicated wildlife garden be? The area I have committed is approximately 175 sq m (of which approximately 30 sq m are occupied by the pond). I have found this just about ideal. In a smaller area, you will find many of the plants are just too vigorous for the whole ever to look really attractive and you will be unable to accommodate all the important features. Remember, too, that in a small garden of any kind, imperfections and mistakes are magnified and become glaringly obvious. Given that a native plant wildlife garden can't ever be wholly neat and tidy, this also becomes especially important if it is very small.

If the area is much bigger than my 175 sq m, it becomes impracticable as part of a domestic garden. (Wildflower meadows are special cases and I deal with them separately, *see p.156*). I was fortunate in one respect. My prospective wildlife area was an old cottage garden that had been neglected for many years. The soil therefore had a low nutrient level, which is important when you are attempting to mimic the natural habitats of native plants that aren't enriched annually by gardeners with packets of fertiliser.

Lowering nutrient levels

In an area like an old vegetable plot with a nutrient-rich soil, native plants will produce masses of foliage but few flowers. More importantly, species like grasses and members of the pea and bean family, such as vetches and clovers that thrive on high levels of nitrogen, will grow so luxuriantly as to swamp everything else. If there is no alternative to such an area, you should try to reduce the nutrient content of the soil. It is sometimes suggested that the nutrient status of a site can be reduced by scraping away the topsoil to expose the impoverished subsoil beneath; but I can only imagine it's suggested by people who have never tried to do it or who have unlimited space to deposit the tonnes they have removed.

A more practical way to remove nutrients from soil is to sow one or more crops of a vegetable with a high nitrogen demand, like a brassica. Space the plants closely (don't apply any more fertiliser) and then remove all the plant matter at the end of the season. If you live in an area of high rainfall, that too will help in washing out soluble nitrogen.

Another way to weaken grass growth, which is useful if you are sowing a grass and wildflower mixture, is to deliberately augment it with seed of partially parasitic plants that will depress the vigour of some of the more aggressive grass species. Yellow rattle (*Rhinanthus*) is the most readily obtained and is offered by many wildflower seed suppliers.

But while I was fortunate that my prospective wildlife area was low in nutrients, it was a mixed blessing that it already had a large population of native plants. There was a rich and extremely vigorous crop of creeping buttercup, field bindweed, stinging nettles, sow thistles, lesser celandine and dandelion, together with substantial populations of groundsel, shepherd's purse, hairy bitter cress, red and white dead nettles, several species of speedwell, and other weeds of

Left Dandelions (*Taraxacum officinale*) and forget-me-nots (*Myosotis*) may have a place in the native plant garden but they are very invasive and need controlling.
Top Red dead nettle is a common annual weed and an excellent bee plant, although it is not in reality a British native but was introduced long ago.
Above Yellow rattle (*Rhinanthus*) can help to depress the vigour of highly aggressive grasses.

cultivation. This highlights the greatest conundrum facing anyone creating a garden of native plants: which are acceptable in the cause of their wider benefit to the wildlife community and which have to be excluded because they will be a confounded nuisance? (For more about the meaning of the term weed in relation to wild or native plants, *see p.199*).

If you have room, have sufficiently good reason, take enough care and are prepared to be strict with your management, I see no reason why any of the perennials among the plants I have just listed shouldn't find space in your wildlife garden. In truth, the only plants I would never have in a wildlife garden, ever, are Japanese knotweed, common horsetail and pink-flowered oxalis but I need to elaborate on my caveats.

By having sufficiently good reason to grow such perennials, I mean the plants must be indispensable for some creature that particularly interests you. You might want to grow stinging nettles as food for the caterpillars of nymphalid butterflies, for example, or dandelions to provide nectar for early-season insects or thistles as food for goldfinches. By taking sufficient care, I mean that the plants should be confined in

sunken containers to control root and rhizome spread – 1m lengths of large concrete drainpipe are ideal – much as mint is controlled on a much smaller scale in a kitchen garden.

By strict management, I mean that you must be prepared to take time annually to weed out the stray plants that will inevitably arise elsewhere in your plot as seedlings (*see p.199*).

Clearing the plot

Even if, as in my case, the existing flora of the native plant area includes species you want to keep, I firmly believe it is sensible to clear the area initially and have as clean a start as possible. The reason I take this view is that the young or seedling plants you introduce will inevitably struggle to grow among established vigorous perennials. In my experience, the only way to clear such an area is by using the weedkiller glyphosate. Digging is of some value, especially on light soils, but on heavy land and with plants such as couch and bindweed that have extremely brittle roots and rhizomes, it is all but impossible to make much impact.

Glyphosate is absorbed by green tissue and translocated or moved down to the roots. It will kill all green vegetation but is inactivated in the soil and therefore offers no residual problems. But you will need to allow the whole of the first year if this is to be really successful. I was fortunate in that first summer being hot and dry – ideal conditions for the weedkiller to work – and we sprayed five times in total.

I am often told that gardeners have used glyphosate and that it doesn't work. It does, and will eradicate most perennials except perhaps horsetail and Japanese knotweed, but it is essential to spray in hot, dry conditions (the official recommendation is that there must be six hours without rain after application in order for it to work properly) and you must repeat it at least twice. Every two weeks is necessary with most deep-rooted perennials.

After about seven days, the weeds stop growing. About seven days later, they begin to show signs of yellowing. That is the cue to spray again. By late summer, my new wildlife area was relatively free of vegetation. A few more spot treatments of the sow thistles, which proved surprisingly more difficult to eradicate than the bindweed, and I felt happy I could safely rotavate ready for the creation of habitats in preparation for sowing and planting.

I do advise you to use a rotavator. If you don't own one, they can be hired inexpensively for a weekend and soon produce a perfectly acceptable tilth, even if you are planning to sow a mini-meadow. Make sure that you hire a proper petrol-engined machine and one with a powered reverse; rotavators are extremely heavy to manipulate and need some practice in steering.

You don't need the thoroughness of preparation required for a lawn. Two passes to about 20cm depth with L-shaped tines, followed by a raking will be perfectly adequate. Some undulations in the surface are in any event attractive.

Creating habitats

In order to obtain the greatest pleasure and variety from your garden and maximise its benefit to wildlife, it's important to create a range of different habitats. Only you can decide what appeals to you and what your site offers. A 175 sq m plot should enable you to produce something that mimics a small area of meadow, a woodland edge (or if there are already established trees, a tiny bit of woodland floor), a cornfield edge, a hedgerow (although if there is none already, this will take a few years to establish), a dry stone wall, a path and path edge, perhaps a small area of dry impoverished rough ground (large loose stones and coarse stone chips in a sunny spot) and of course the pond and pond edge. The position of the pond should dictate the position of everything else because its requirements are the most strict (*see p.180*).

If your plot is smaller than 175 sq m, you will need to reduce the number of habitats accordingly – don't try to do too much or you risk jeopardising the usefulness all of them.

Above If you plan to have a pond, decide on its site first, before any other habitats.

Introducing the plants

There are three main ways to plant an area of native plants. You can sow or plant individual plants or species; you can sow or plant individual species into an overall sowing of wild grasses, or you can use a 'wildflower' seed mixture of both grasses and wild flowers. The latter two are better courses for most mini-habitats.

In my experience, when sowing or planting individual species into a sowing of wild grasses, or using wildflower seed mixtures, you must be prepared to adjust, adapt and modify to obtain the best results. Several seed firms now specialise in native plant seed mixtures. The major component of each mixture is grass, to which seed of more or less appropriate wild flowers have been added. Typically, they are called meadow mixtures, wild flower mixtures, woodland mixtures, or pond-edge mixtures. The drawbacks of these ready-made mixtures is that they may not contain your favourite wild flower, the suppliers may not describe which grasses they

include, and the packet often contains too much ox-eye daisy (*Leucanthemum vulgare*). I have no real objection to ox-eye daisy, even considerable quantities of it, in meadow or even hedgerow mixtures but I can't be convinced it should be a major component of woodland or water-side blends as it sometimes is.

One solution is to contact a wildflower seed supplier and buy their grass mixture without any wild flowers (although not all will supply this). You can then buy individual plant species separately and so produce your own mixture. Clearly, to do this meaningfully requires a working knowledge of the native plants that inhabit the environment and I indicate in the course of this section some of my own recommendations. And, of course, for some of your mini-habitats, such as 'wasteland', dry stone walls and paths, grasses may be insignificant components and you will need to buy seed of each flower species individually.

Even with the 'meadow' blends based on grass, you have a difficulty in that without experience, it is hard to choose the optimum proportions – just how much ribwort and ragged robin seed do you need to ensure it won't all be swamped by the grasses? A useful compromise is to discover from the seed suppliers' catalogues the proportions used in the various ready-prepared mixtures and either add or leave out individual species to blend your own. There is one point to stress. You must use a grass mixture blended for the purpose.

Left Meadow barley (*Hordeum secalinum*), one of the grasses that can be added to your wildflower mix.

wn seed simply won't do; at least coarse lawn seed
n't do because it is largely composed of vigorous
rid rye grasses that are most unattractive and lank
when in flower. The grass blend I have used extensively
(*see box, below*) is a good benchmark to use if you are
blending your own. On certain sites, some grass species
will germinate better than others and in places with
particularly unusual features (like the wet pond edge)
you will want to add one or two but I find it much
easier to use the same grass mix throughout and vary
the types of wild flowers to add to it (*see pages 158–61*).

Sowing rates are about 4–5g per sq m of a grass and
wildflower mixture or 1g per sq m for native flowers
alone. As with any broadcast sowing, it's important to
use a 'filler' to obtain uniform distribution. I use sawdust
in a ratio by volume of about 50 parts sawdust to one
of seeds. Whenever possible try to sow in late summer;
before September will give the best early germination
followed by good establishment in the following year.

Right A mixture of meadow grasses
and verbascums.

Recommended grass seed blend

Species	Percentage
Crested dogtail *Cyanosurus cristatus*	35 per cent – this is a lovely grass and is almost always a major component of native grass mixtures
Red fescue *Festuca rubra*	25 per cent
Common bent *Agrostis capillaris*	10 per cent
Small timothy *Phleum pratense*	10 per cent
Crested hair-grass *Koeleria macrantha*	5 per cent
Meadow barley *Hordeum secalinum*	5 per cent
Quaking grass *Briza media* **[right]**	5 per cent
Sweet vernal grass *Anthoxanthum odoratum*	5 per cent

The wildflower meadow

Following years of herbicide use, traditional wildflower meadows had all but disappeared from the landscape. Now, their floral diversity is being encouraged once again but there is a long way to go. By creating your own miniature meadow, you can enjoy the extraordinary beauty of a bygone era in your own garden.

No aspect of growing native flowers evokes as much interest and nostalgia as the wildflower meadow. Although my post-second world war generation can still remember the nature and characteristics of the real old farm hay meadows with their extraordinary and beautiful mixtures of grasses and flowering plants, succeeding generations who grew up in the late 1950s and 1960s were brought up to think of meadows simply as areas of grass, their floral diversity effectively sterilised by the liberal use of selective herbicides.

In a parallel way, so the roadside verge, another truly beautiful habitat when left more or less to its own devices, was chemically sprayed and mown to become a barren wasteland. There has been a reversal of this trend in more recent times by some farmers in relation to hay meadows and by practically all local authorities in relation to verges. But progress is slow, and so even today, a miniature garden meadow will evoke huge interest and give much pleasure.

In practice, there is little difference other than in scale between a small meadow area in a native plant garden such as mine and something of an acre or more. And whilst an acre is certainly a big garden, country gardeners may find themselves the owners of a paddock or small field, which offers a good opportunity to create something larger. You will need farm machinery to prepare and manage it, but establishment and management are governed by just the same rules as in a small garden plot. In large measure, you can choose whatever grass and wildflower mixture appeals to you, but it is helpful to know the approximate pH of your soil because some mixtures are intended for chalk or limestone sites. And if your land is particularly heavy, it is sensible to choose a blend containing species that will germinate easily in clay soils.

In my own garden, on soil that is neutral, I subdivided the meadow area with stepping stone paths and sowed each of the four segments with a different blend. In time, as seeds are dispersed from one segment to another, the differences become blurred but I have been surprised how, ten years on, each still has its own floral identity. My four mixtures were all based on my basic grass seed blend (*see p.155*) in the proportion of 80 per cent by weight grass mix and 20 per cent by weight flower mix. I have called them Garden Meadow, Shady Meadow (for the area slightly overhung with trees), Heavy Meadow (for an area that comprised a patch of heavy sub-soil brought to the surface), and Chalky Meadow. I believe one or other of these will be suitable for most garden situations in Britain.

Managing your meadow

Much more than any other part of your wildlife garden, a wildflower meadow needs managing. Left to its own devices, it will soon become an unsightly tangle as old foliage and stems drop and rot in situ and soon it will be neither use for your wildlife nor ornament for you.

You need to emulate farmers with real meadows and remove a crop of hay each year. The timing is all-important as the plants must be left standing until the seeds have set and then, after cutting, the residue must be left and turned on the ground for a few days to dry fully and to ensure the seeds are shed.

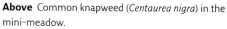

Above Common knapweed (*Centaurea nigra*) in the mini-meadow.

Above right A mixture of vetches (*Anthyllis*) in the meadow in summer – these have gradually become more prominent over the years.

Take your interest in wildflowers further:

Wild Flowers, John Akeroyd (Collins, 2004)
Meadows, Christopher Lloyd (Cassell, 2004)
www.thewildflowersociety.org.uk – national society for wild flower lovers and amateur botanists
www.wildflowers.co.uk, *www.wildflower.org.uk*, *www.organiccatalog.com*, *www.wigglywigglers.co.uk* – suppliers of wild flower seeds and plants

Wildflower meadow seed mixtures

HEAVY MEADOW wildflower seed mix	% by weight
Ragged robin *Lychnis flos-cuculi*	1
Devil's bit *Scabious*	2
Wild teasel *Dipsacus fullonum*	5
Self heal *Prunella vulgaris*	5
Purple loosestrife *Lythrum salicaria*	5
Cowslip *Primula veris*	10
Red campion *Silene dioica*	20
Meadowsweet *Filipendula ulmaria*	22
Meadow buttercup *Ranunculus acris* **[right]**	30

CHALKY MEADOW wildflower seed mix	% by weight
Yarrow *Achillea millefolium*	1
Kidney vetch *Anthyllis vulneraria*	3
Clustered bellflower *Campanula glomerata*	3
Greater knapweed *Centaurea scabiosa*	3
Wild carrot *Daucus carota*	6
Lady's bedstraw *Galium verum*	6
Rough hawkbit *Leontodon hispidus*	6
Birdsfoot trefoil *Lotus corniculatus*	6
Wild marjoram *Origanum vulgare*	6
Selfheal *Prunella vulgaris*	6
Ox-eye daisy *Leucanthemum vulgare*	8
Ribwort plantain *Plantago lanceolata*	8
Cowslip *Primula veris* **[right]**	8
Meadow buttercup *Ranunculus acris*	10
Salad burnet *Sanguisorba minor*	10
Small scabious *Scabiosa columbaria*	10

GARDEN MEADOW wildflower seed mix	% by weight
Betony *Stachys officinalis*	1
Yarrow *Achillea millefolium*	2
Ragged Robin *Lychnis flos-cuculi*	3
Salad burnet *Sanguisorba minor*	3
Rough hawkbit *Leontodon hispidus*	3
Lady's bedstraw *Galium verum*	8
Ox-eye daisy *Leucanthemum vulgare*	8
Wild carrot *Daucus carota*	10
Common knapweed *Centaurea nigra*	10
Ribwort plantain *Plantago lanceolata*	10
Self heal *Prunella vulgaris*	12
Field scabious *Knautia arvensis* **[right]**	15
Meadow buttercup *Ranunculus acris*	15

SHADY MEADOW wildflower seed mix	% by weight
Dog's mercury *Mercurialis perennis*	2
Foxglove *Digitalis purpurea*	5
Agrimony *Agrimonia eupatoria*	5
Pendulous sedge *Carex pendula*	6
Ox-eye daisy *Leucanthemum vulgare*	8
Cow parsley *Anthriscus sylvestris*	8
Jack-by-the-hedge *Alliaria petiolata*	8
Bluebell *Hyacinthoides non-scripta*	8
Wood avens *Geum urbanum*	8
Meadow sweet *Filipendula ulmaria*	8
Hedge bedstraw *Galium mollugo*	10
Red campion *Silene dioica* **[right]**	12
Common knapweed *Centaurea nigra*	12

Below An attractive meadow mix that includes poppies (*Papaver rhoeas*), cornflowers (*Centaurea cyanus*) and toadflax (*Linaria vulgaris*); Californian poppies (*Escholzia californica*) provide a welcome splash of orange but would be out-of-place in an exclusively native meadow.

Right An orchard meadow seen at the 'magic hour', with the sun dipping in the evening sky, makes for a spectacular sight, as the different flowers and grasses are picked out in vivid detail.

Cutting the meadow

The time of the harvest varies from season to season but I usually try to cut during August or at the beginning of September. Much the best tool to turn the cut hay is a pitchfork but no-one seems sure what to use to cut it down initially. Lawn mowers are hopeless, scythes wonderful in theory but for them to be effective you need an incredibly sharp blade, a very dry crop and the biceps of an 18th century farm labourer. Strimmers make a mess, slashing the material rather than cutting it and throwing pieces in all directions. Allen scythes are excellent for large areas and a tractor-mounted mower is essential for fields. But I have never read an account of anyone having a satisfactory answer for mini-meadows like mine.

Several years ago I discovered the perfect solution. Now I wouldn't dream of operating a wildflower meadow without it. I use a long-handled hedge cutter with a two-stoke engine. The shaft is about 120cm long and the adjustable blades add another 60cm and can be turned at any convenient angle to the handle. It's a big piece of equipment but used with a sling, it's certainly

Above The author uses his long-handled hedge cutter to cut the meadow to approximately 20cm above soil level on a dry day in early autumn.

not anything like as much hard work as when it is being held upright to cut tall hedges.

The blades are interchangeable and the manufacturers now produce a ground-cutting version with a tough shielded back to prevent blade damage when the machine is used right at soil level. Although the blades are shorter, I find the ground-cutting version perfect however for keeping pathways clear through the meadow during the growing season. I don't pretend that these hedge cutters are cheap but for me they are quite indispensable.

I cut the meadow to about 5cm above soil level on a warm dry day, although if the vegetation is at all damp, it I find easier to cut it twice – first to about 20cm and then lower at the second cut after it has had a week or so to dry. When cutting your meadow, be careful not to chop down any sedges (*Carex* species) or rushes (*Juncus* and *Luzula* species) you may have. They are typically, although not exclusively, plants for wet places and are most likely to be present in pond edge seed mixtures or to have been planted at the pond side individually (*see p.186*). The Cyperus sedge (*Carex pseudocyperus*) for example, is an easy to grow pond-edge plant that looks attractive all year round. But these plants are much less adept at regenerating from the base than grasses and herbaceous meadow perennial flowers. By leaving them, you will also give the area some height and interest during the winter.

After the hay has dried and the seeds have been shed, it should be raked into heaps for composting. I confess I was at first daunted by the quantities produced, even from my small area, and I had doubts about how easily it would break down in the compost bin without being shredded. In the event, I found it degrades extremely well within 12 months although it is especially important not to allow the compost bin to dry out.

Creating paths through a meadow

It is very important to have paths through a meadow. By early summer, the vegetation will be a metre or more high and you won't be able to stroll through it and enjoy the plants unless you make pathways. This can be done informally, simply by regularly mowing strips across it but I took the more permanent course of laying stepping stone paths across the whole area as soon as the ground had settled after rotavating and before I sowed (*below*).

There are several advantages to this. The stones served to divide the area into discrete sectors for sowing, they allow access close to the pond for viewing without any risk of the pond edge being damaged, and of course they mean the pathways don't become unacceptably muddy even in wet weather. Stepping stone paths themselves also offer yet another habitat opportunity. Because they are walked on regularly and mowed weekly during the summer, they provide an environment for plants that are naturally tolerant of grazing and trampling.

In time of course, selection means that such species would invade naturally. I decided to help things along, however, by sowing the paths with self heal (*Prunella vulgaris*) and wild thyme (*Thymus vulgaris*). Although they have to fight their corner against plantains and some of the clover family, especially white clover (*Trifolium repens*), lesser trefoil (*Trifolium dubium*), and black medick (*Medicago lupulina*), on the whole it has worked well.

Cornfield edge

If you sow cornfield annuals with your meadow seeds, there may be flowers in the first season but second generation plants stand no chance among established perennials. Cornfield annuals, like garden annuals, need a space to grow free from competition from perennials and an area that mimics a cornfield edge is ideal.

Gardening magazines and newspapers often come with packets of 'wildflower seeds' attached as free gifts but the instructions accompanying them are generally sparse. It's not made clear that by sowing the seeds you won't have a wildflower meadow; and you may not have anything at all the following year unless you take some care.

The packets almost invariably contain a mixture of seeds from a group of plants that have become known as 'cornfield annuals' – wild flowers that have adopted the habitat of cereal fields where they grow (or grew before the advent of selective weedkillers) as extremely attractive weeds.

By far the most common are the bright red field poppy (*Papaver rhoeas*), the beautiful lavender-coloured corncockle (*Agrostemma githago*), the blue corn flower (*Centaurea cyanus*), white corn chamomile (*Anthemis arvensis*) and golden yellow corn marigold (*Chrysanthemum segetum*).

Another interesting plant sometimes included in the mixtures is pineapple weed (*Matricaria discoidea*), a small, rather fleshy weed with green knob-like flowers. It's a member of the daisy family although it has none of the characteristic petal-like ray florets but is attractive to birds which feed on the seeds. It is an introduced species and is now widespread by paths and in areas of waste land.

It is well worthy of a place in the native plant garden although it isn't especially typical of cornfields. In fact, I am a bit puzzled why it is included in the mixes since in my experience, it is quickly overshadowed by the taller species. I have an area of about 15 sq m along one

Below Pinkish-purple flowers top tall slender stems of corncockle in the author's cornfield edge habitat in summer.

side of the wildlife garden that does just this. Rustic posts, three strands of wire and some old gate posts complete the illusion and add to the interest – the gate posts are much favoured by hibernating insects and as perches by birds on their way to collect seeds from the ground. In one sense, the area is treated in the same way as the meadow – the sowing takes place in late summer, and the dead top growth is cut down at the same time the following year.

Sowing and management

My initial sowing was of a mixture comprising by weight approximately 15 per cent each of field poppy, corn marigold and corncockle, 35 per cent cornflower and 30 per cent corn chamomile. There are two important differences from the meadow, however. Over the years, I have found that whilst corncockle and, to some extent, field poppy will produce sufficient viable seed to regenerate themselves without my help, the others gradually disappear, either through there being insufficient seed produced or because the seedlings are swamped by the corncockle. I therefore augment the supply by sowing fresh seed each autumn.

The second difference is that unlike native perennials, cornfield weeds need fertiliser – after all they grow naturally in one of the most highly fertilised places in the country. Without a handful of fish, blood and bone fertiliser each season, the plants are feeble and prone to suffer from competition with bigger weed species.

In order to make the area even more attractive and 'authentic' I also sow a few handfuls of cereal seed – wheat, barley, oats, rye – each year. I have been interested to see that at least one native plant seed supplier has begun to do the same thing and offer a mixture of cornfield annuals plus cereals.

The only other management necessary is to keep a careful watch for seedlings of any vigorous perennials that spread in from other parts of the garden or from outside (birds will regularly do their best to add to your native plant population by carrying in seeds). It's

Above A mixture of cornfield annuals – yellow corn marigold, blue corn flower and lilac corncockle.

very important that you dig them out in the spring. I find a long-handled spiked weeding tool ideal for this and I remove any intruders at the same time as I am thinning out the dandelion population (*see p.199*).

Dry stone wall

Extremely valuable as habitats for a huge number of plants, animals and lower organisms, dry stone walls are constructed from stones without any mortar to bind them together and rely on a special method of construction to hold them up. Fortunately, you don't need to be a craftsman to build your own 'field boundary'.

I have always been fascinated by the fauna and flora of walls; especially dry stone walls such as those that criss-cross the landscape of my native county of Derbyshire. But as I no longer live in dry stone wall country and to have one as a garden boundary would be both ridiculous and anachronistic, I have created the simplest of replicas in my wildlife garden. It is a feature that gives immense pleasure; and on the evidence I have seen, performs a valuable service, too.

Covering an area of only about 8 sq m, my replica represents the end of an old dry stone wall where it abuts a large gate post. A few of the component stones remain in situ with the others having fallen down. I bought a load of appropriate angular boulders ranging in size from a few centimetres to 35–40cm in diameter and arranged them accordingly.

I prepared a sieved mixture of garden compost and soil in roughly equal amounts by weight, added seeds of as many wall-inhabiting native plants as I could find and sprinkled, pushed and poked it into the multitude of holes. Some species germinated and grew well. Some, like herb Robert (*Geranium robertianum*), became

Left The author's tumble-down wall is home to a variety of wall-inhabiting native plants.

Above Among the species at home on this dry stone wall are maidenhair (*Asplenium*) and hart's tongue (*Phyllitis scolopendrium*) ferns, cranesbills (*Geranium*) and a fine assortment of mosses and lichens.

reliably self-perpetuating. Some, like wallflowers, (*Erysimum cheiri*), I saw for one year but not again. Some, like ivy-leaved toadflax (*Cymbalaria muralis*), I never saw – its seed appears notoriously tricky to germinate 'to order' despite it being such a common plant in the wild. I supplemented the seed sowing by inserting plants of a few additional species like the fascinating fleshy leaved navelwort (*Umbilicus rupestris*) and generally these too thrived.

Around the fallen boulders I introduced seed or plants of other species such as common toadflax (*Linaria vulgaris*), lady's bedstraw (*Galium verum*) and hedge bedstraw (*Galium mollugo*). These, too, survived well although I carefully cut back any invading grass

or other vegetation from the nearby mini-meadow that threatened to swamp them. White dead-nettle (*Lamium album*) seems to have a predilection for the base of the wall and is a valuable plant for bees and other insects but it needs carefully to be kept in check.

The only difficulties arise in hot dry summers when some plants find survival difficult although I have to say that I have lost almost no species; individuals have gone but their seeds, fallen into cracks and crevices, have renewed the population the following year.

Some native and naturalised plants for growing on walls or in wall cavities

Flowering plants	Comments	How to establish
Biting stonecrop *Sedum acre*	Can be invasive but forms masses of pretty yellow flowers	Use small plant fragments
Common toadflax *Linaria vulgaris*	Delightful yellow flowers; for sides and base of wall	Seed or plants
Feverfew *Tanacetum parthenium*	Choose the true wild form, not the sickly yellow cultivated variety	Seed or plants
Greater celandine *Chelidonium majus*	Yellow flowers on stems up to 80cm; for large walls only	Seed
Herb Robert *Geranium robertianum* [1]	Annual, scrambling wiry stems and tiny red flowers	Seed
Ivy-leaved toadflax *Cymbalaria muralis*	Purple and yellow flowers on soft trailing stems	Plants
Maiden pink *Dianthus deltoides*	Neat cushions of pink flowers, for top of alkaline walls	Plants
Navelwort *Umbilicus rupestris*	Rounded, fleshy leaves and short spikes of green-white flowers	Plants
Red valerian *Centranthus ruber* [2]	Red flowers on stems up to 80cm; for large walls only	Seed or plants
Snapdragon *Antirrhinum majus*	Wild forms usually have pinkish-purple flowers	Seed
Thrift *Armeria maritima*	Pink flowers, neat cushions on top of wall	Plants
Wallflower *Erysimum cheiri*	Biennial; wild forms usually have orange flowers	Seed

Ferns	Comments	How to establish
Black spleenwort *Asplenium adiantum-nigrum*	Best on damp wall sides	Plants
Hart's tongue *Phyllitis scolopendrium* [3]	Best in damp crevices at wall base	Plants
Maidenhair spleenwort *Asplenium trichomanes*	Best in damp wall sides; some forms are intolerant of lime	Plants
Polypody *Polypodium vulgare*	Once established, tolerates dryness on top of wall	Plants
Rusty back *Ceterach officinarum*	Alkaline walls, best in cavities in sides	Plants
Wall rue *Asplenium ruta-muraria*	Best on wall sides with alkaline rocks	Plants

Waste land

It may strike you as rather strange to suggest that a small area of waste land be deliberately incorporated into a wildlife garden. Yet it allows you to grow some interesting and extremely attractive species and so provide appeal for a further group of creatures that feed on, and shelter among them.

There are, of course, many kinds of waste land but the mini-habitat I have created attempts to mimic the type of environment found, say, on a lowland scree or a railway embankment. It is very free-draining and impoverished of nutrients.

To create my miniature waste land of about 9 sq m, I dug a hole approximately 30cm deep and filled it with a mixture of soil and rubble. On top, I laid a 6cm deep layer of large coarse limestone chips, approximately the size of railway ballast.

Having left it over winter to weather and settle, it was planted and sown in spring with a range of small species, mainly annuals which self-seed, including the beautiful yellow-flowered common toadflax (*Linaria*

Left Rosebay willowherb is one of the most familiar plants that colonise waste land such as old railway tracks where the soil is free-draining but impoverished.
Above Sticky groundsel (*Senecio viscosus*) is a common waste ground coloniser.

vulgaris), small toadflax (*Chaenorhinum minus*), common corn salad (*Valerianella locusta*), common whitlow grass (*Erophila verna*), sticky groundsel (*Senecio viscosus*) and also several of the smaller willowherbs including spear-leaved willowherb (*Epilobium lanceolatum*) and short-fruited willowherb (*Epilobium obscurum*), which

in turn have now become infected with interesting species of rust fungi. Spiders, a number of different ground beetles and, more surprisingly, some woodlice and millipedes clearly find the area appealing.

I obtained confirmation that the habitat was a passable imitation of what I intended when that archetypal waste-ground plant rosebay willowherb (*Chamerion angustifolium*) colonised naturally. This also served to stress, however, that a wildlife garden needs management – the intruding plants were just too aggressive for their companions and had to be persuaded to move elsewhere!

Woodland

Creating a woodland habitat in your garden can be a challenge because it requires trees – in the plural. A single tree doesn't constitute a small wood, although five or six in a group might. If you succeed, however, you may attract numerous wood-dwelling creatures, as well as help protect declining plant species.

Even with the requisite trees, creating a mini-woodland presents another problem – one that becomes apparent if you look at the plant life in a real wood. It's what is called a discontinuous habitat – there are scattered bits of plant life with their associated fauna here and there with areas of bare ground in between. It isn't like a meadow which, although not uniform, is continuous.

The reasons for this discontinuity are two-fold. First, the amount of light reaching down through the trees to soil level varies across the wood depending on the types of tree, their size and how close they are to one another. And second, the trees drain the soil of moisture and nutrients so, overall, some places are more conducive to plant life than others. A small group of trees in a garden is unlikely to create major problems with respect to the amount of light reaching soil level – unless they are all large, dense conifers – but the soil beneath them will very probably be dry. For this reason, alone among all my native plant mini-habitats therefore, I sometimes have to supply additional water to the 'woodland'. I do this by having a sprinkler hose pegged down in a zigzag fashion across the area.

Supplying water on a few occasions in summer and applying plenty of additional leaf mould in winter has ensured that a good population of woodland plants thrives. I have found, however, that it is optimistic to expect seeds to germinate and practically all my woodland flora originates from putting in groups of plants. Particularly successful, interesting species that have established well in the shadiest spots are dog's mercury (*Mercurialis perennis*), deadly nightshade, (*Atropa belladonna*), moschatel (*Adoxa moschatellina*), wood anemone (*Anemone nemorosa*), wood sorrel

Left In the author's woodland edge habitat, meadow plants like meadow buttercup (*Ranunculus acris*) gradually give way to more shade-tolerant species like foxglove, red campion and dog's mercury.

(*Oxalis acetosella*), cuckoo pint (*Arum maculatum*), wood cranesbill (*Geranium sylvaticum*) and, eventually, bluebell (*Hyacinthoides non-scripta*). Bluebells are strange plants because they usually spread easily and rapidly once established but they aren't easy to start from seeds. And on the subject of bluebells, do please choose the native bluebell, not the introduced Spanish bluebell (*Hyacinthoides hispanica*). The Spanish bluebell is an aggressive, invasive plant that ousts the native plant both by direct competition and more subtly by hybridising with it. This is one of the most important and dramatic examples of genetic pollution by a species escaping from gardens into the wild in Britain.

A small number of grasses have been successful too, especially sweet vernal grass (*Anthoxanthum odoratum*) and wavy hair grass (*Deschampsia flexuosa*). Additionally, I have planted a small number of woodland shrubs and climbers including holly (*Ilex aquifolium*), guelder rose (*Viburnum opulus*), spindle (*Euonymus europaeus*), honeysuckle (*Lonicera periclymenum*) and bittersweet (*Solanum dulcamara*); and, judging by the number of holes nibbled in the leaves, most are playing a significant part in the local ecosystem.

Plants that require slightly higher light levels will thrive at the 'woodland edge'. Among my successes here are wild strawberry (*Fragaria vesca*), primrose (*Primula vulgaris*), wild daffodil (*Narcissus pseudonarcissus*), yellow archangel (*Lamiastrum galeobdolon*), sweet woodruff (*Galium odoratum*), foxglove (*Digitalis purpurea*), which is a marvellous bee plant, and red campion (*Silene dioica*). Some of these plants are equally at home in hedgerows and, if I had more room, I would include important but invasive species like ramsons (*Allium ursinum*), often incorrectly called wild garlic, and cow parsley (*Anthriscus sylvestris*).

Above The tubular flowers of the foxglove are perfectly adapted to allow foraging bees access to the nectar and pollen.
Right The native English bluebell is under threat from the invasive and aggressive Spanish bluebell, both by direct competition and hybridisation.
Overleaf A traditional English bluebell wood.

Hedgerow

Around 300 species of British plant commonly grow in hedgerows, sometimes almost to the exclusion of anywhere else. By creating a wildlife hedge in your garden you are providing a hugely important habitat that should also be highly rewarding for you as you watch it grow and develop.

If you don't have any hedges in your wildlife garden, try to plant one as soon as possible (*see p.100* for information on common hedging plants). For dedicated wildlife interest, I strongly recommend a native plant hedge comprising predominantly hawthorn with additional selections chosen from blackthorn (*Prunus spinosa*), yew (*Taxus*), hazel (*Corylus*), beech (*Fagus*) and holly (*Ilex*).

Among these, plant odd specimens of other valuable wildlife shrubs such as dog rose (*Rosa canina*), which is important for many insects, and elder (*Sambucus nigra*) whose white flowers are attractive to insects and the fruits an important bird food. Include buckthorn (*Rhamnus cathartica*) and alder buckthorn (*Frangula alnus*) as well, since they are the food plants of the brimstone butterfly.

Left A spring hedgerow with hawthorn (*Crataegus monogyna*) in blossom and meadow buttercups.
Right Hedgerow plants, including red campion, cow parsley and dog's mercury.

If you are planting a new wildlife hedge, plant it within your garden to create a sub-division rather than at the margin. This is because a dedicated wildlife hedge won't necessarily make the most effective or neat garden boundary. Pulling out some plants and replacing them with others or leaving the hedge in an 'untidy' state may not have equal appeal to everyone. If there is an existing hedge in your wildlife garden that forms a boundary to your property and you want to adapt and manage it specifically for wildlife, first make sure that you own it and then discuss your plans with your neighbour.

With a new hedge, a double line of plants will provide a better, denser, habitat. It's important to help the hedge establish as quickly as possible and so, unlike the rest of the wildlife garden, plants should be given fertiliser and thickly mulched for some years. Don't introduce hedgerow perennials in the early stages; it's much more important to build up a healthy hedge structure first.

If you are in a position to adapt an existing hedge that is largely or wholly made up of exotic and relatively uninteresting plants like cypresses or Japanese privet, give serious thought to replacing some of them. This isn't necessarily easy or cheap because well-established hedge plants can be tenacious, although conifers are unlikely to be deeply rooted. To fill the gaps successfully with more worthy native species, you will need to buy relatively large plants. Prepare new planting holes thoroughly with compost and fertiliser and don't allow the plants to dry out while they become established.

Managing a wildlife hedge

There are two important aspects to managing a wildlife hedge. First, the manner and frequency with which it is cut can have a remarkable effect on its wildlife value. Research has revealed that while leaving hedges unclipped approximately doubles the numbers of birds roosting and nesting, actually leaving bits sticking out increases by five fold or more the numbers of individual birds and also increases the number of species. Of course, it's impractical to leave a hedge unclipped, as it will soon became huge, unsightly and possibly illegal. Clip it once a year, therefore, after the birds have fledged, and leave some unclipped branches protruding. These can be left for one or two years before being removed for their place to be taken by others.

The second aspect to hedge management relates not to the top but the bottom. I've alluded already to the importance of striking a balance between being too scrupulous in removing hedge bottom debris and in leaving so much that it affects the hedge's growth. For the dedicated wildlife hedge, only the ground flora and debris that appear significantly to be affecting the growth of the hedge should be thinned out. It's vital not to disturb the soil layer itself where rodents, other mammals and legions of invertebrates have their homes and where fungi, mosses, liverworts and lichens grow.

Alongside the base, if not actually beneath the hedge itself, a characteristic hedgerow flora can and should be encouraged. Some will arrive of their own accord; others should be planted. There are some species that immediately reveal in their names their natural affinity for this habitat – Jack by the hedge (*Alliaria petiolata*), hedge parsley (*Torilis*), hedge woundwort (*Stachys sylvatica*) and so forth – but there are many others, too. (See *p.178* for a range of perennials and a few annuals to try.) They won't thrive in all hedges but the proportion that do so will enhance a hedge's appearance and significantly improve its wildlife benefit.

Valuable hedgerow flora

Name	Notes
Cleavers *Galium aparine*	An annual with remarkably tenacious clinging fruits, which attach themselves to fur and clothing. It soon becomes rampant and will drape itself over the entire hedge but it has the most slender of roots and can easily be pulled out by the armful and kept in check
Hedge bedstraw *Galium mollugo*	Tiny white flowers and typical *Galium* whorled leaves. An important food plant of numerous moths, including several species of hawk moth
Common dog violet *Viola riviniana*	Delightful little purple flowers – this is an important food plant for most species of fritillary butterflies
Cow parsley *Anthriscus sylvestris*	One of the most characteristic flowers of late spring, its white umbels attract large numbers of pollinating insects
Cuckoo pint **[1]** *Arum maculatum*	Attracts interest because of its curious flower structure in spring – a club-like spadix of minute flowers surrounded by a sheath-like enveloping spathe. Bright red fruits produced later in the season are eaten avidly by mice, voles – and slugs
False oat grass **[2]** *Arrhenatherum elatius*	A tall, oat-like grass with shining flower heads
Ground ivy *Glechoma hederacea*	Small lipped mauve flowers and ivy-like leaves. A good ground-cover plant sheltering numerous insect species. The leaves can cause skin irritation

Name	Notes
Hedge woundwort *Stachys sylvatica*	Like a tall, slender red dead nettle with coarse leaves and a strong aroma. The food plant of the rosy rustic (*Hydraecia micace*) and the plain golden Y moths (*Autographa jota*)
Hogweed *Heracleum sphondylium*	Tall, white-flowered umbellifer with broad, toothed leaflets. Food of the white-spotted pug (*Eupithecia tripunctaria*), garden dart (*Euxoa nigricans*) and brindled ochre moths (*Dasypolia templi*)
Ivy *Hedera helix*	Can strangle hedges if allowed free rein but forms invaluable wildlife cover at the base. If some is grown to full height, it will flower – resulting black fruits are highly attractive to many birds. A food plant of the holly blue butterfly (*Celastrina argiolus*) and several moth species
Jack by the hedge *Alliaria petiolata*	Small white flowers in spring and a garlic smell. An important food plant for the most beautiful of all spring butterflies, the orange tip (*Anthocharis cardamines*)
Stinging nettle *Urtica dioica*	The food plant of some of the most beautiful butterflies including peacock (*Inachis io*), small tortoiseshell (*Aglais urticae*), red admiral (*Vanessa atalanta*) and painted lady (*Cynthia cardui*)
White bryony *Bryonia dioica*	A scrambling plant with tiny green-white flowers and red fruits that attract birds when other food is scarce
Wild hop [3] *Humulus lupulus*	This scrambling plant must be cut back hard at the end of the season. The fruits are used to flavour beer. Red admiral and comma caterpillars feed on it, as do several moth species

The wildlife pond

The principal objective of a dedicated wildlife pond is to attract wildlife, unlike a 'normal' garden pond, which is an ornamental feature that looks attractive but where wildlife benefit is a bonus. A wildlife pond should also feature exclusively native plants – both within the pool itself and around its margins.

The siting of a water feature, especially a pond, is critical. You can't simply put one anywhere that takes your fancy and expect it to be attractive and to function properly. The reason is that sunlight is crucial – the position should have as close as possible to eight hours of direct illumination each day, although this needn't apply to the whole of the surface area. Provided half or even a third of the surface area has full exposure to the sky, this will be adequate.

There is no minimum size (as I mention on *p.143*, ponds can be created in old barrels) but to make a serious contribution to wildlife and to your garden, it really should have a surface area of more than 20 sq m and be at least 45–60cm deep. My wildlife pond is irregular in shape but has a total area of approximately 30 sq m, the deep end is 1m, shallowing to 60cm over the rest of the area but with a 20–25cm deep ledge of varying width all the way round.

Constructing the pond

A modern pond in a modern wildlife garden is best constructed using a butyl 'rubber' liner. Puddled clay and concrete linings are rarely used nowadays and while pre-formed plastic liners are widely available and easy to install as formal ponds, they are impractical for large pools. They also constrain you to a pre-determined shape and depth and aren't easy to disguise.

For most gardeners, I recommend butyl rubber therefore, but please don't economise on your choice. Buy the best you can afford as there must be few

greater frustrations than finding your newly established pool has sprung a leak because you bought a thin or otherwise inferior liner. Pond liners vary principally in the thickness of the butyl rubber sheet although they are often priced according to the length of the guarantee – which can vary from about five years to 'a lifetime'.

Much unwise advice has been given about the installation of pond liners. No matter how thick it is, a liner can be punctured by sharp objects, so some form of underlay is essential to protect it from flints or debris in the soil. No matter how carefully you check the inside of the hole, small objects can still be missed. Placing the liner on a layer of sand is often suggested but I don't recommend it. Laying sand down the vertical sides is all but impossible and in a garden where the water table may be fairly near the surface during heavy winter rain, sand will very soon dissipate from beneath the liner and the protection will vanish.

Some people advise using old carpet as an underlay. If the carpet is polypropylene or other plastic and very flexible, it might succeed. If it contains any wool or other natural fibre, it won't, because the structure will be lost as the natural material slowly rots. There is no effective and reliable alternative to purpose-made proprietary fleece underlay. It is easy to handle, flexible, durable and relatively inexpensive and I always use it in a double layer.

Having placed underlay and liner in place with plenty of overlap at the sides, slowly fill the pond with a hose. The liner will take up the strain and stretch to fit the hole as you do so although I find it helps to ease it into

Top left The author's newly excavated pond with a 1m deep end, shallowing to 60cm, and a 25–30cm deep shelf.

Top right The edges of the liner are anchored and concealed by soil, which has been overlaid by high-grade lawn turf.

Bottom Pebbles and paving slabs are used to attractively disguise the liner where it overlaps the pool.

place with a soft broom. At first, you will probably be horrified at the appearance of your creation. It will be shiny, obvious, unashamedly artificial and look nothing remotely like the lovely water feature you saw in your mind's eye. Banish these concerns. Black pond liners are easy to disguise and nature will help too.

Once the pond has filled with water and the liner has finished stretching, the edges need anchoring and concealing. Dig a narrow trench and tuck the edges of the liner into it, firming the soil as you back fill. It will be very difficult to persuade soil to stay in place over the top of the liner while seeds germinate in it, so the best plan is to lay turf. Be sure to choose high grade lawn turf without rye grass and then, once it has established, you can make holes in it for pot-grown pond side plants – but be careful not to slice through the edges of the liner with your trowel as you do so.

Where the liner overlaps the edge of the pool, use pebbles to conceal the plastic and help provide further security. Don't skimp on the use of pebbles – you can buy them in bags relatively inexpensively and they certainly look very attractive in the months before they gradually disappear from view as vegetation colonises on the pond sides and algal growth conceals them below the surface.

In fact the entire liner will 'disappear' within a year due to the overgrowth of algae and encrustations of mineral deposits. The liner in my wildlife pond, folds and all, is now practically indistinguishable from submerged rocks. I find it helps to scatter sieved soil over the pebbles to which the seed of pond-side plants has been added. This will fall down the numerous gaps and crevices and some will germinate.

Among the seeds I sowed successfully at the edge of my pond were meadow sweet (*Filipendula ulmaria*), creeping Jenny (*Lysimachia nummularia*), water forget me not (*Myosotis scorpioides*), water mint (*Mentha aquatica*) and watercress (*Rorippa nasturtium-aquaticum*). You may also want to sow a proprietary pond-side selection close to the pond to abut against the turf edge but my experience is that these are the least successful of the various packeted wildflower mixtures. Germination is often poor and erratic.

Above Watercress (foreground) provides spawning areas for frogs and newts.
Right The wildlife pond surrounded by lush growth in spring.

Oxygenating the water

The key to the success of garden ponds is adequate oxygenation. And adequate oxygenation is achieved much the most easily by movement of the water. Like most other gardeners, I read and was told that the way to oxygenate water is 'the natural way' – using oxygenating plants. These are more or less totally submerged plants that, like other green vegetation, give off oxygen through their leaves. Instead of this dispersing into the atmosphere as it does with terrestrial species, the oxygen passes into the water to help create a suitable environment for fish, other forms of aquatic life and other plants. It's a good theory but it doesn't work in practice because self-evidently there isn't enough oxygen. And in any event, I don't believe it is the natural way. Look at any natural expanse of water and find one if you can where there is vigorous aquatic life, none of the foul smells that are symptomatic of anaerobic decay — and no water movement. Rivers and streams patently have water movement for oxygenation and lakes have streams running into and out of them. So do many ponds; even if the flow is in a culvert or below the surface and not immediately apparent.

Occasionally, you will find a totally isolated pond with no water flow either in or out that is apparently healthy; but it is probably so utterly choked with aquatic vegetation that it is scarcely a thing of beauty;

and any fish or other aquatic life is all but invisible. So if it won't do in nature, it won't do in gardens. Yes, there should be submerged oxygenating plants in your pond but they should be there to provide places for fish and other aquatic creatures to hide and breed. The maxim for a healthy, vigorous garden pond is to ensure that it is oxygenated because the water moves - and moves all year round.

Water movement in a formal pond is achieved most commonly and easily with some type of fountain. Air is dragged into the water as it splashes back and so the pond is agitated and simply and efficiently oxygenated. The fountain, or at least the jet from it, is nonetheless

often far too big and both visually and functionally wrong. It's easy to over-cool the water, especially in a small pond, by setting the fountain jet too high, too wide or simply by having too many of them – rather like the rose on a watering can.

In a wildlife pond, you can have a fountain squirting upwards if you wish but I find it looks anachronistic. I have the fountain spout, without a rose attachment, protruding just above the surface to give a bubbling rather than spraying effect. The flow rate of the pump is such that the equivalent of the entire volume of water in the pond should pass through the pump in about 48 hours.

Many gardening books, in their monthly calendars of jobs, recommend cleaning out the fountain pump in late autumn and putting it away for the winter. That, too, is unsound advice. Clean out your fountain pump in autumn by all means, but put it back in the pond, not in the garden shed. In all but the hardest frosts, an area of water will remain unfrozen so any gases from decomposing matter in the pond can escape, oxygen can enter – and local birds will be guaranteed somewhere to drink.

Submerged plants

One of the first basics that any prospective water gardener learns is that plants for the water garden fall into a number of distinct categories that require significantly different treatments, in effect depending on how great is their demand for a truly aquatic environment. And this is as true for native plants as for exotics. At one extreme is a group I have already mentioned – the submerged (oxygenating) plants that live entirely or almost entirely submerged, sometimes hardly even rooted in the pool mud and rising above the water surface only to flower, if at all. Most species of submerged plants found in garden ponds are exotics,

many are highly invasive and some are so invasive that their sale is now restricted. None of them need concern the native plant gardener, who can choose from two relatively innocuous British species with finely feathered leaves – rigid hornwort (*Ceratophyllum demersum*) and spiked water milfoil (*Myriophyllum spicatum*). You could also include the rather more vigorous Canadian waterweed (*Elodea canadensis*). Although introduced, it has been naturalised for nearly 200 years and while at one time, it was invasive and problematic, the populations sold now appear to be much less aggressive.

You should at all costs avoid a South American relative of water milfoil called parrot's feather (*Myriophyllum aquaticum*), which has caused major problems by obstructing waterways.

The most seductively lovely of submerged plants is the native common water crowfoot (*Ranunculus aquatilis*), a white-flowered water buttercup with grass-like submerged leaves and celery-like floating ones. It is widely offered for sale and although it grows naturally in ponds and slow-moving water, I find it is never very successful in captivity. It has close relatives that live only in the fast-flowing, clear current of natural streams, their roots anchoring them with astonishing tenacity into the bed. I have yet to satisfy myself how newly emerged seedlings achieve their initial foothold in what is often a torrential flow.

Left Water crowfoot has lovely white buttercup flowers.

Should I buy pond snails?

A lot of nonsense is talked and written about snails in ponds. It is said that snails are essential 'to keep the pond clean' by consuming algae, fish faeces and the like, and that you should buy some accordingly. I have never bought pond snails and my ponds are full of them. They arrive on water plants and as eggs attached to birds' feet. I'm sure they're an important part of the aquatic ecosystem but, in my experience, they don't make any difference to the clarity, appearance or general health of the water.

Floating plants

Floating plants are those that simply float. Some have no roots and some have roots that dangle into the water but none are anchored in any way. They die down in the winter to survive as dormant buds, resting in the mud of the pool floor to grow and rise again with the arrival of warmer conditions in the spring. Like some submerged plants, many exotic floating plants multiply vegetatively with great rapidity and in consequence, can cause serious problems if they are allowed into rivers, canals or other water courses.

The most common native floating plants are our three native species of duckweed and I think I am in a significant minority in welcoming them in my pond. I have two of the species, fat duckweed (*Lemna gibba*) and the even tinier common duckweed (*Lemna minor*). I find them most attractive, they provide important shade and shelter for aquatic creatures and they can be contained by frequent netting. Sadly, my native plant pond is also home to one of the invasive aliens, the extraordinarily beautiful but extraordinarily vigorous floating fern known as water fern or fairy moss (*Azolla caroliniana*). It requires frequent netting to contain it, although in one way I take its presence as an indication that my pond has been a success in that it attracted a pair of mallard who brought it on their feet.

The group I call basic water plants are those that grow within the pool, away from the edge and anchored in the mud but with leaves and flowers arising to float at the surface or be raised above it. All are best and most conveniently planted in purpose-made planting baskets. It is a large and diverse group, although there are few good native species apart from the tall, angular, spiky but rather appealing branched bur-reed (*Sparganium erectum*).

But the classic water plants are water lilies. There are two native species. The yellow-flowered brandy bottle, (*Nuphar lutea*), is the one you don't want, at least not unless you have a lake. It is huge and has the largest leaves of any British plant. Much better is the white water lily (*Nymphaea alba*). Although it is often said to require water 1-2m deep and to spread up to 2m across, that shouldn't put you off. I have mine in a sunken terracotta 20cm-diameter pot. It grows in 60cm of water and thus confined is perfectly manageable and produces a succession of flowers each year.

Marginals

Plants that grow at the edge of the water are called marginals. Among native species, the group covers plants with a range of habitat requirements such as bog bean (*Menyanthes trifoliata*), a spreading, almost scrambling plant with large, three-lobed, broad bean-like leaves and small white, star-like flowers, that must exist permanently in a few centimetres of water. It also includes plants like arrowhead (*Sagittaria sagittifolia*) that tolerate periodic drying out of the water's edge, and those like the beautiful giant 'buttercup', the marsh marigold (*Caltha palustris*), that need really saturated, waterlogged soil but preferably not standing water.

Above The native white water lily (*Nymphaea alba*) contained within a submerged terracotta pot.
Far right Purple loosestrife (*Lythrum salicaria*) thrives at the edge of a pond.

Marginal plants to avoid

· ·

Because marginal plants come into such intimate contact with the pool liner, particular care is needed both in their selection and their planting. Some have strongly growing, invasive and, most importantly, sharp rhizomes that will readily puncture the sheet and initiate a leak. Top of the list of those to avoid are the several species of reedmace (*Typha*) – sometimes popularly called bulrushes – which have needle-like rhizome tips and are in any event far too vigorous for most small pools.

Left Wasp-pollinated water figwort beside the author's pond with ox-eye daisies (*Leucanthemum vulgare*) in the background, in the first year after sowing.

Water plantain (*Alisma plantago-aquatica*) is a valuable and attractive marginal species, very appealing to insects and producing feathery seedheads later in the summer. It is sometimes said to be a problem through self-seeding but I have never found this so. One or other of the aquatic species of horsetail, water horsetail (*Equisetum fluviatile*), marsh horsetail (*Equisetum palustre*) or perhaps best of all, rough horsetail (*Equisetum hyemale*) will also make a fascinating addition to the pond – like most marginals, they can equally successfully be planted in submerged baskets at the water's edge.

For adding height and providing all-year interest (its old flowered shoots make a sculptural feature right through the winter) one of my favourite marginals is water figwort (*Scrophularia auriculata*), a tall, branched plant with small purple-brown flowers that have the additional interest of being wasp-pollinated.

Among the most valuable and also most versatile of marginals is watercress (*Rorippa nasturtium-aquaticum*). It will grow in wet water-side mud as well as in the water at the pond edge from where it spreads with floating leaves and floating roots into the open water. It provides a superb habitat for frogs to lay their spawn but must be cut back from time to time if it threatens to venture too far from the shore. At the pond edge it intermingles with the blue-flowered aquatic speedwell called brooklime (*Veronica beccabunga*) and the dainty water buttercups, the greater and lesser spearworts (*Ranunculus lingua* and *Ranunculus flammula*).

Bog gardens

· ·

Marginal plants grade almost imperceptibly into the plants of the bog garden, the most varied of all water garden habitats and one that is highly important for wildlife. At one extreme in the bog garden are the plants only one step removed from the marginals themselves and that need extremely wet soil. They are what I might usefully call conventional bog garden species – plants such as marsh cinquefoil (*Potentilla palustris*), one of the most attractive of all members of the cow parsley family, the introduced but well naturalised sweet cicely (*Myrrhis odorata*), the beautiful water avens (*Geum rivale*)

Below left Sweet cicely is a very attractive bog garden plant.
Below right, top The flower and leaves of the beautiful water avens.
Below right, bottom The European globe flower is the original wild species from which cultivated varieties have beeen bred, but is no less charming than its garden cousins.

with its nodding rust-red and yellow flowers, and globe flower (*Trollius europaeus*), a lush and luxuriant member of the buttercup family so attractive to early season insects. At the other end of the spectrum are those species requiring moisture-retentive soil but which are intolerant of real waterlogging. Many of them never receive a mention in most water gardening books as they are considered merely border perennials but I believe the more informal type of water garden that include a bog garden, should grade gradually into the other, drier parts of the remainder. Among the more unexpected native plants I have in mind here are such perennials as bugle (*Ajuga reptans*) and catchfly (*Lychnis chalcedonica*).

But if bog gardens and bog plants in general don't receive the attention and interest they really merit,

there is one group of plants that is all but ignored. How often do you hear of a bog shrub or a bog tree? Yet walk alongside any river, stream, pond or other natural water course and you will almost invariably be in the company of at least some woody plants. It's true that not many water-side trees are suitable for gardens, partly because most grow rather tall but mainly because the quantity of deposited foliage (even from evergreens) will be more than the volume of water can absorb without being fouled. But small wetland shrubs are another matter and I find them especially valuable in providing height in the bog garden and close to the water's edge, particularly during the winter.

The best wetland shrubs benefit from acidic soil, such as pink-flowered bog rosemary (*Andromeda polifolia*) which I have fund curiously and unexpectedly tolerant of considerable dryness, perhaps an adaptation to living in acidic soils that dry out in summer. There is the lovely brown-flowered bog myrtle (*Myrica gale*) or, in strongly acid conditions, even species of *Vaccinium* like the cowberry (*Vaccinium vitis-idaea*) or bog bilberry (*Vaccinium uliginosum*).

All these species are the food plants of a wide range of interesting moths, although unless you live in an area where there are significant local populations, it is expecting too much to hope you will necessarily attract them.

Building a bog garden

To construct a bog garden, what's needed is an area of soil that is permanently wet but not too wet – I sometimes remind gardeners of the difference between a bog and a swamp. By my definitions, a bog has more soil than water, a swamp the reverse. On a heavy soil in a region of high rainfall and a natural or artificially dug hollow (especially at the foot of a slope), such a thing may arise naturally. Nonetheless, even here it can't be relied on to stay permanently wet enough, especially with the increased frequency of warm, dry summers that climate change promises. With my light soil, more or less flat garden and our fairly low rainfall, it would be even more chancy. The answer is to dig out a hollow, exactly as you might for a pond but 30cm – or at most 45cm – deep.

Line it with the cheapest pond liner you can obtain (or even at a pinch, old plastic bags) and punch some holes in it. Before backfilling, you need to ensure as much continuity of water supply as possible and I achieve this by channelling the rainwater from the greenhouse and other nearby garden buildings through pipes laid in shallow trenches.

Place the outlet of the pipes in a pocket of coarse gravel (to prevent soil from blocking the end) and then refill the hole, adding a quantity of organic matter as you do so.

Left Excavations under way in the author's bog garden, showing the water supply channel.

Choosing fish

Most pond owners will want to stock their pond with ornamental fish but in a wildlife pond, you will find they exist to the detriment of much other aquatic life, especially amphibians. I have found this doesn't seem nearly as relevant with native fish, however, but here nonetheless, you should choose carefully. Small to medium-sized fish, appropriate to pond rather than river life and not permanently living at the bottom of the pond are appropriate. In my own pond I have minnows (*Phoxinus phoxinus*), three-spined sticklebacks (*Gasterosteus aculeatus*) and most successful of all, rudd (*Scardinus erythrophthalmus*). Tench are sometimes suggested but they are bottom-living fish – they will simply churn up the mud and you never see them.

The species I recommend can generally be obtained (often to special order) from specialist aquatic suppliers. If you want to net a few fry from your nearest river or lake, you will need permission – from the landowner and the owner of the fishing rights and also a permit from the Environment Agency under the Salmon and Freshwater Fisheries Act, 1975.

One important rule is not to feed native fish but allow them to live naturally and eat what food they find naturally. This means they will never grow too large and there is nothing cruel about this. Most fish vary widely in size depending on the available food source – you only need compare the wild brown trout of mountain streams with the huge bloated creatures in fish farms to see the evidence of this. The only disadvantage is that by keeping them small you will probably find the fish may not breed in your pond: my rudd and minnows have never bred, although the sticklebacks have.

Further information and resources for creating a pond:

Water Gardening, Graham Clarke (Collins, 2004)
The Pond Specialist, A. & G. Bridgewater
  (New Holland, 2004)
www.pondstrust.org.uk – website of Ponds Conservation, offering practical advice on the conservation of ponds
www.english-nature.org.uk/Nature_In_The_Garden
  – for a downloadable pamphlet on 'Garden ponds and boggy areas'
www.pondplants.co.uk, *www.blagdonwatergardens.co.uk*,
www.aquatics-direct.co.uk, *www.bradshawsdirect.co.uk*
  – suppliers of pond equipment and aquatic plants

KEEPING YOUR WILDLIFE GARDEN HEALTHY

Gardening in a way that promotes the wellbeing of wild creatures doesn't mean your garden will be immune from pests and diseases. And wanting to conserve interesting wild plants doesn't mean that weeds will ignore you. To garden in a meaningful and enjoyable way, you will need to exercise some control.

I've already suggested that simply calling yourself an organic gardener and using chemical products that organic gardeners use isn't necessarily the best way forward. In this chapter I want to look at pest and disease control that uses only natural processes and at other non-chemical ways of keeping your garden healthy.

First, I shall look at an option that is often called biological control – mimicking or enhancing the ways that pests are controlled naturally. Unfortunately, there are no biological control methods currently available for diseases, at least in gardens.

Biological controls

The range of biological pest controls available to gardeners has increased significantly in recent years and I have summarised the most important in the table (*right*). Those I find the most valuable, relatively easy to use, widely available and effective are listed first but for gardeners used to controlling pests with a chemical spray, it's important to realise that biological controls aren't cheap, they generally need fairly precise conditions (especially temperatures) in which to work optimally and, in most cases, they aren't quick to act. Moreover, most of the important types can only be used in greenhouses. That said, I do believe they represent the way forward and the range of options available is increasing all the time.

Above Ladybird larvae are just as valuable as adult ladybirds in terms of pest control – they, too, feed on aphids.

Biological control can also be used slightly differently – not by artificially introducing a new creature to your garden or greenhouse but by encouraging those already there. This approach has its greatest benefits outdoors, although the results aren't easily quantifiable. The creatures that are especially amenable to this sort of encouragement all feed on aphids – ladybirds, hoverfly larvae and lacewings. But how do you encourage such free spirits to accumulate in your garden, apart from having a population of aphids to lure them? First, take advantage of the fact that, in general, yellow flowers are rather effective in attracting insects, hoverflies especially. Placing a few bright yellow flowers – marigolds (*Tagetes* and *Calendula*) are among the easiest and most reliable – among vegetables or other plants vulnerable to aphids can be helpful. You can also encourage these predatory insects by supplying them with places to shelter or hibernate. Ladybird and lacewing boxes are sold for this purpose – although I confess my own experience with them is equivocal. I still find greater numbers of ladybirds in their more traditional over-wintering places beneath loose bark and in the crevices of fence posts than I do in their purpose-made homes.

Effective biological controls

Pest	Biological control organism	Use and limitations
Greenhouse whitefly	*Encarsia formosa* (a tiny parasitic wasp)	In a greenhouse at a minimum air temperature of 18°C
Red spider mites	*Phytoseiulus persimilis* (a predatory species of mite)	Best in a greenhouse at a minimum air temperature of 10°C
Vine weevil (larvae)	*Heterorhabditis megadis* (an eelworm that carries bacteria)	Outdoors at a minimum soil temperature of 12°C
Mealy bug	*Cryptolaemus montrouzieri* (a predatory ladybird beetle)	In a greenhouse at a minimum air temperature of 20°C
Some soil pests (including vine weevil)	*Steinernema carpocapsae* (an eelworm that carries bacteria)	Outdoors at a minimum soil temperature of 14°C
Slugs	*Phasmarhabditis hermaphroditica* (an eelworm that carries bacteria)	Outdoors at a minimum soil temperature of 5°C
Aphids	*Aphidoletes aphidimyza* (a predatory species of midge)	In a greenhouse at a minimum air temperature of 10°C
Aphids	*Aphidius matricariae* (a tiny parasitic wasp)	In a greenhouse at a minimum air temperature of 10°C
Aphids and other pests	*Chrysoperla carnea* (a species of lacewing)	Greenhouse/outdoors at a minimum air temperature of 10°C
Scale insects (soft scale only)	*Metaphycus helvolus* (a tiny parasitic wasp)	In a greenhouse at a minimum air temperature of 22°C
Fungus gnats	*Hypoaspis miles* (A predatory species of mite)	In a greenhouse at a minimum air temperature of 12°C
Thrips	*Amblyseius cucumeris* (a predatory species of mite)	Greenhouse/outdoors at a minimum air temperature of 10°C
Greenhouse whitefly	*Delphastus pusillus* (a predatory ladybird beetle)	In a greenhouse at a minimum air temperature of 15°C

Protecting your plants

Plants can be protected from some pests by purely physical methods. Fruit cages, lightweight netting and similar procedures are especially valuable in the kitchen garden (see *p.119*) for protection from birds. Fine mesh netting and barriers will also protect vegetable brassica crops from large white butterflies.

Use prickly twigs around slug susceptible plants like lettuces and plastic 'fencing' around carrots. This improbable technique depends on knowing that female carrot flies remain fairly close to ground level and a barrier of plastic sheeting approximately 60cm high around the carrot bed will stop many of them on the barrage balloon principle.

Simple traps may work for some pests, too, although great care is needed as they tend to be non-discriminatory and kill harmless species along with the pests. Small sunken traps filled with beer are reasonably safe for catching slugs however; my experience is that woodlice are the only other creatures lured at all commonly by the smell and sweetness. Home-made or proprietary traps with covers to prevent rain diluting the beer or other creatures drinking it are the best.

Below Netting protects brassicas from large white butterflies.
Right These yellow marigolds (*Tagetes*) are good at attracting aphid-eating insects.

Disease resistance

Apart from these fairly crude methods and using natural parasites and predators, pest and disease control without chemicals is essentially a matter of avoidance. It falls into three main categories – growing resistant varieties, adjusting your cropping times and what I like to call garden hygiene.

Most good nursery and seed catalogues indicate varieties that have resistance to, immunity to, or tolerance of important pests and diseases. Not all resistance by any means is absolute and the subject is complex because many diseases exist as different strains, some of which affect certain varieties but not others. Moreover a variety that is tolerant of disease (as opposed to resistant) will still be attacked by it but will show no effects whilst nonetheless remaining a symptomless 'carrier' of the problem for infection of varieties that aren't tolerant. None of this is intended to put you off; merely to explain that whilst choosing a disease-resistant variety is an excellent idea, you should not be too disappointed if it doesn't offer a complete solution. Among many important diseases for which there are reasonably good resistant varieties are Michaelmas daisy mildew, rose black spot and rose rust, antirrhinum rust, parsnip canker, lettuce downy mildew, potato blight and tomato wilt. Significantly good resistance exists to several pests and important examples are varieties resistant to carrot fly, lettuce root aphid and potato eelworms.

Alteration of the sowing or planting time of vegetable crops can sometimes be effective in avoiding problems. The theory depends on trying to avoid having plants at a susceptible stage of development at a time when there are pests available to attack them. The sowing of pea crops to ensure that the plants aren't in flower in June and July when the pea moth is laying its eggs is one example, while early potato crops often escape the worst effects of slug damage because the slugs haven't had time to build up before the potatoes are harvested. In heavily slug infested soil, you may find you need to abandon growing maincrop varieties.

Far left Environmentally friendly earwig traps. The insects crawl up to hide in the straw in the daytime, when they can be collected. **Left** A cut-off plastic bottle and strip of copper tape give a young seedling double protection from slugs.

Good garden hygiene

Keeping the garden tidy and free from places where pests and diseases may lurk can play a part in limiting the impact of pests and diseases but it's important to strike a balance between keeping the plot healthy and having a garden that is so sanitised it offers no places for any wildlife to live. Leaving annual flowers and vegetables in the ground once they have fulfilled their purpose (including their value as bird food, *see p.116*) is inviting trouble, however, and they should be cleared away and composted. Whilst piles of logs are important and valuable for sheltering small creatures in the wilder parts of a garden, woody debris, including prunings, shouldn't in general be left among growing plants as it will encourage pests and some diseases, too.

There has never been much justification for using chemical weedkillers in a garden, although I don't believe every type of weedkiller should be excluded as a matter of principle. For annual weed control, a fork (large and small) and a Dutch hoe are all you need. Use the hoe in warm dry weather so the weeds shrivel quickly. With a few species, like groundsel, where the seeds continue to mature even after the plants have been chopped down, you should rake them up and compost them.

Perennial weeds in established beds and borders can be controlled similarly provided they are dealt with regularly – it is when they have been left long enough to establish a deep root system that problems arise. Even then, careful and concerted digging should be adequate. The real difficulties occur when a garden is over-run with deep-rooted or far-creeping perennial weeds such as bindweed, creeping thistle, couch or, one of the most underrated, perennial sow thistle. Here I see no objection to using the translocated weedkiller glyphosate to clear the area initially. It is degraded in the soil and will then enable you to begin gardening as you would wish.

Covering weed-infested areas with black plastic sheeting to deny weeds light and so starve them is often advocated. I have never been able to achieve significant results in any less than three years on ground that is badly infested with deep-rooted weeds, which is longer than most gardeners will want to see their plot both

Above Use a garden fork to remove stubborn perennial weeds.

unsightly and unproductive. Flame guns may have a small part to play but their literal scorched earth technique will inevitably kill many small creatures along with the weeds and weed seeds.

The wildlife greenhouse

The notion of a wildlife greenhouse may seem something of a contradiction. Wildlife is all about the great outdoors and a greenhouse provides an unnatural environment in which to grow out-of-season, exotic and alien species. But a greenhouse can still be run on wildlife-friendly principles.

The same values, arguments and justifications apply to plant raising, propagation, feeding and watering in a greenhouse as are relevant in the wider garden. Pest and disease control however is a bigger challenge. The warm, sheltered greenhouse environment that cossets our plants cossets pests and diseases, too, but given that chemical pesticides are not to be used, what options does it leave?

The first and, for disease control, much the most important, is air movement. Plant diseases, by and large, are caused by fungi and the conditions in which

fungi thrive are dampness and stagnant air. Ventilators, preferably working automatically on the principle of a wax-containing tube that expands as temperature rises, will ensure fresh air is allowed to enter while at the same time ensuring that the interior of the greenhouse doesn't overheat.

Better still is to add a fan that will keep the air circulating. In a small greenhouse, it can be the same fan heater used for winter warmth but with the heating elements turned off. In my own large heated greenhouse, I use a ceiling fan for the same purpose and despite the deliberately very high humidity, diseases are almost non-existent.

Below Good ventilation is vital in a greenhouse to avoid damp, stagnant conditions in which diseases thrive.

Pest control

Environmentally friendly pest control offers several options. Sticky yellow cards will trap flying creatures although inevitably some good will be trapped along with the bad. A second option is to use biological control. I have mentioned that greenhouses are the ideal environment for biological control organisms which are more likely to stay put and not fly off to the wide world outside (*see p.192*). All these procedures involve using one small species of invertebrate to control another but there are larger possibilities.

My large greenhouse is home to a very big common toad that found its way in as an infant, soon grew too large to get out by the way he entered and has stayed, both to his and my contentment, dining on whatever ground-living pests he can find. A small colony of his

Above The North American green *Anolis carolinensis* lizard is pretty, but it is likely to climb up a greenhouse and escape.

exotic relatives the European tree frog (*Hyla arborea*) is also a permanent greenhouse feature. These delightful creatures are noisy at night but generally unseen in the canopy of plants where they dine on insects.

I also have a small population of lizards, which fulfil a similar purpose although more obviously. For preference I would have chosen our native common lizard or one of its European relatives like the wall lizard (*Lacerta muralis*) which as a boy I kept in the days when they were readily obtainable.

Now, rightly, only captive bred animals may be sold and these species don't breed freely in captivity. Instead I have turned therefore to North America and the *Anolis* lizards which do breed readily. I first tried the prettiest, the green *Anolis carolinensis* but it showed a surprising

propensity to climb the sides of the greenhouse, with almost the virtuosity of a gecko. This enabled the lizards to escape though the only open exits, the high roof vents. Having investigated *Anolis* ecology, I discovered that while the green species lives naturally in the forest shrub layer and up to the tree canopy, its near-relative, the brown *Anolis sagrei* fills a different niche, living in the shrub layer and down towards the ground. Although less attractive, it very satisfactorily and visibly helps maintains pest control in the greenhouse while showing no wish to climb upwards and escape.

Compost, recycling and wildlife

The environmentally friendly principles of recycling must surely go hand in hand with a wish to garden for the benefit of wildlife. Recycling is second nature to many gardeners. It's called composting. Here, I describe the best way to make compost and the special importance it has for the wildlife gardener.

In all except the smallest gardens, you will need two items of equipment - a compost bin and a compost shredder. Without a powered shredder, I don't believe you can make good compost and you certainly can't utilise all the waste from any except the smallest garden. A shredder will chop up almost all woody garden debris but it isn't the fact that it chops wood that makes it so useful. It is simply the fact that it chops. Even relatively soft herbaceous material will decompose better when it is slashed into smaller fragments because the greater the surface area in relation to the volume, the more effectively and quickly the bacteria and fungi in your compost bin will be able to decompose them.

There are many models on the market, most powered by electricity but some, especially the largest, by petrol engines. The bigger, most powerful machines are fairly expensive but cost isn't usually a prohibiting factor for people who hesitate over a purchase. Nor are running costs. There are two things that really concern people and the noise these machines generate is one of them. In some countries noise pollution is taken so seriously that there are restrictions on the times in the week that powered garden machinery of any sort may be used.

I don't deny that shredders are noisy, although European legislation means noise reduction is now the most important factor for manufacturers and with quieter (and more efficient) engines and various ingenious sound-deadening devices, today's modern machines are immeasurably less intrusive than their predecessors. But legislation or not, I would still urge all gardeners to use them on days and at times when they will cause the least offence to neighbours; and try to shred small quantities regularly, rather than allowing waste to accumulate and then finding it takes all day to deal with it.

Left Garden waste decomposes much more quickly if it is shredded.
Right A purpose-built wormery is effective if you have small amounts of waste organic matter.

Choosing a compost bin

Compost is made in a compost bin, an enclosed but well-aerated structure, not in a heap. Small, plastic barrel-style containers with plenty of holes in the sides are fairly effective and can be useful for the smaller garden. Some are mounted on pivots so they can be tumbled to provide extra aeration and ensure the contents are thoroughly mixed.

So-called wormeries, too, have their uses. The name originated about 50 years ago to mean a structure or place for breeding worms rather than one for producing compost but in recent times small models have been manufactured for gardeners' use. In essence, a wormery in its present sense is a small, self-contained compost maker that depends for its action on an abnormally large number of earthworms, introduced artificially.

They are only effective if you have very small quantities of waste organic matter, such as household vegetable scraps, and will only provide sufficient compost for tiny gardens. That is not to decry them; converting waste to compost in a wormery is far better than throwing it away and because the chamber separates into a number of sections, it is easy to see how the whole operation works and they are invaluable as educational tools for children.

But wherever space permits, I recommend strongly that you use a slatted wooden bin of about 1m cube. Best of all is a double bin; one side can be filled while the other matures. After air, the most important ingredients for successful compost making are a source of nitrogen to encourage bacterial action, and water. The nitrogen is best applied as fresh farmyard or stable manure for every 15-20cm of compost that is added. If this isn't practicable, a proprietary compost 'accelerator' powder containing nitrogen should be sprinkled over the organic matter. If the bin is carefully sited, natural rainfall will keep it moist and additional watering should only be needed in the driest of weather. Almost inevitably, the bin will be positioned in a corner of the garden and a fence or overhanging branch may provide sufficient shelter to prevent waterlogging. If not, then a coarse plastic net over the top will be helpful.

For composting fun, start here:

Create Compost, Pauline Pears (Impact Publishing, 2004)
How to Make Soil and Save Earth, Allan Shepherd
    (CAT Publications, 2003)
www.gardenorganic.org.uk – for downloadable factsheets
www.communitycompost.org - website of Community
    Composting Network
www.wigglywigglers.co.uk, www.organiccatalog.com
    – suppliers of compost bins, wormeries, activators
    and shredders

Because leaves break down so much more slowly than most other organic matter, they are better stacked separately in a leafmould cage, made of small mesh chicken wire netting secured to corner posts, again making a structure of about 1.2m cube. Large leaves, like those of horse chestnut, need to be passed through the shredder first.

Ideally, the compost in the bin should be turned at least once. This will ensure that all the debris has the opportunity of experiencing the highest temperatures that arise in the centre. In practice, it is easiest to turn material about three weeks after it has been added – turning the contents of an entire bin is physically almost impossible. Compost should be ready to use after about six months although the upper quarter or so of the contents may be inadequately decomposed by that time and so should be transferred to a second bin or used to start the first one afresh. As compost making is the essence of recycling, it's important to compost as much material as possible. I think gardeners should be able to recycle 95 per cent of garden-related material in their own gardens and then leave the remaining 5 per cent to the local authority. I also think that a proportion, perhaps 10 per cent, of household waste can be recycled in gardens – although I accept that all of this arithmetic and calculation applies to people with gardens big enough for at least one compost bin and access to a garden shredder.

Starting with the simplest garden waste – lawn mowings and similar soft green matter – these need no further treatment and can go straight to the bin. Some apparently soft matter, like windfall apples, are best chopped or shredded because the fruits have thick, waxy protective skins and will simply emerge after nine months in the compost bin as recognisable apples, not recycled mush. Some vegetable stems, especially brassicas, really need pounding before they will degrade. Brussels sprouts stalks, in particular, are like tree trunks – I dry them and then treat them like any other woody matter; which means they go through the shredder.

Left (clockwise from top) A mesh chicken wire compost bin is ideal for leaves; a rustic woven frame used as a leafmould cage; and a triple slatted wooden bin – ideal for the large garden with lots of waste to compost.
Right A ready-made plastic compost bin is fairly effective for the smaller garden.

If you have a small garden and a small amount of twiggy matter such as prunings, you can cut them into small pieces and they will break down fairly well for recycling; larger quantities must be shredded. But bear in mind that to work properly and efficiently a compost bin needs to contain a blend of material. So although I say that lawn mowings need no further treatment, they do need to be alternated in the bin with coarser, tougher matter or they will stick together in wet soggy masses.

Recycling paper

What of the five per cent of garden waste that I don't think anyone can recycle at home? This material is mainly plastic – wrappings, old plant pots and seed trays – together with glass bottles and metal. It can and should be recycled; but by someone else.

I think the biggest domestic problem in garden recycling relates to paper. For paper to degrade and be recycled, it must be shredded, otherwise, the flat sheets simply adhere together and block up the flow

Left Paper shreds mixed with chopped-up windfalls and stalks in the compost bin.
Below Compost is the perfect mulch; place it on bare soil in early autumn or spring.

of water and air through the compost bin. The bulk of what I call normal postal paper can be dealt with using a small office shredder. Newspapers are a problem: domestic paper shredders won't deal with them and nor will garden compost shredders, which simply clog, so I think they are better left to the professionals. Many local authorities have a waste paper collection service. Cardboard is also tricky. Small amounts can be cut manually into pieces but here, too, the best plan is to flatten it and take it to the local recycling centre.

What about the contention that most recycling is a waste of effort because as much energy is used up in doing it as is saved by reusing the material? I'm not sure. I can see the merits of the argument but something has to be done with waste material and alternative methods of disposal (like burying it in big holes) also use energy; although for no return whatever.

The merits of compost (and leafmould) production for the wildlife gardener fall into two separate parts – the material itself and the place where it is made. There is good reason to cover the bare soil of all your permanently planted areas with compost. Provided it is put on in autumn or early spring when the soil is moist, it will help to retain that moisture, it will suppress annual weeds and it will also help protect against the penetration of hard frosts.

It will also most importantly provide a habitat for enormous numbers of insects and other invertebrates and these in turn will attract the creatures that feed on them – birds especially. It might be infuriating when blackbirds scratch compost over your paths and lawn but do be persuaded that it is all performing an invaluable function. As worms drag the organic matter into the soil, it will help maintain good soil structure and will replenish the nutrient reserves in the most natural way possible.

In dedicated wildlife gardens or beds of native plants, this will provide more than enough for their total needs. Never forget, however, that in beds of cultivated flowers as well as fruit and vegetables, expectations are higher and the demands the plants make on the soil nutrient reserves are higher so some supplementary feeding with fertilisers will be needed.

The finishing touches

Just as in any other garden, the dedicated wildlife garden should be furnished with additional features to attract and benefit wildlife. The natural nesting places you have provided for birds should be supplemented with bird boxes and bird feeders (*see pp.56–57*). There should also be at least one bat box (*see p.62*) and boxes to appeal to insects (*see p.70*).

But because of the different nature of a wildlife garden, you have scope for other, less neat and tidy features, too. At least one pile of logs will provide hiding places and habitats for many small creatures. I have several in different spots, including one beneath the trees and one at each corner of the path through my mini-meadow. I also have logs at the edge of the pond, with one end dipping into the water.

In using log piles, avoid the temptation to keep peeping underneath! If you want to look occasionally, just tip a log briefly to one side. I have piles of both hardwood and conifer logs because different kinds of fungi, wood-attacking insect, moss and liverwort may well grow on and in the different types of wood. If you don't have a dry stone wall habitat, have a loose pile of rocks. Some creatures prefer to shelter in them because they tend to be warmer than logs.

WILDLIFE GARDENER'S REFERENCE

Hopefully this book has stimulated your interest in many different aspects of wildlife gardening and, by now, you are eager to take it further and find out more. In this final section I have therefore provided a selection of recommended further reading in the various subject areas explored in this book. Also included are contact details for a host of different gardening and wildlife organisations where you will be able to gain further information, discover places to visit and find out about activities and campaigns that are happening.

Further reading and Resources

Further reading

WILDLIFE
General
Bill Oddie's How to Watch Wildlife, Bill Oddie, Stephen Moss and Fiona Pitcher (Collins, 2005)
Collins Field Guide: British Wildlife Sounds, Geoff Sample (Collins, 2006)
Collins Wild Guide: British Wildlife (Collins, 2005)
Fauna Britannica, Stefan Buczacki (Hamlyn, 2005)
Natural History of Selborne, The, Gilbert White (many editions)

Birds
Collins Bird Guide, Svensson et al. (Collins, 2001)
Collins Field Guide: Garden Bird Songs and Calls, Geoff Sample (Collins, 2001)
Collins Wild Guide: Garden Birds, Stephen Moss (Collins, 2005)
Secret Lives of Garden Birds, The, Dominic Couzens (Christopher Helm, 2004)
Understanding Bird Behaviour, Stephen Moss (New Holland, 2006)

Fungi and lichens
Collins Wild Guide: Mushrooms and Toadstools, Brian Spooner (Collins, 2005)
Mushrooms, Roger Phillips (Macmillan, 2006)
New Naturalist: Fungi, Brian Spooner and Peter Roberts (Collins, 2005)

Insects and other invertebrates
Britain's Butterflies, David Tomlinson and Rob Still (WILDGuides, 2002)
Bumblebees, Christopher O'Toole (Osmia Publications, 2002)
Collins Field Guide: Spiders of Britain and Northern Europe, Michael Roberts (Collins, 2001)
Collins Field Guide to the Caterpillars of Britain and Europe, David Carter (Collins, 2001)
Collins Wild Guide: Butterflies and Moths, John Still (Collins, 2005)
Collins Wild Guide: Insects, Bob Gibbons (Collins, 2004)
Complete British Insects, Michael Chinery (Collins, 2005)
Enjoying Moths, Roy Leverton (Poyser, 2002)

Field Guide to the Dragonflies of Britain and Europe, Klaas-Douwe B Dijkstra and Richard Lewington (British Wildlife Publishing, 2006)
Field Guide to the Moths of Great Britain and Ireland, Paul Waring and Martin Townsend (British Wildlife Publishing, 2003)
Ladybirds, Darren J, Mann (Osmia Publications, 2002)
New Naturalist: Bumblebees, Ted Benton (Collins 2006)
New Naturalist: Ladybirds, Michael Majerus (Collins 2006)
Red Mason Bee, The, Christopher O'Toole (Osmia Publications, 2000)
Spiders in the Gardens, Dr Rod Preston-Mafham (Osmia Publications, 2003)

Mammals
Bats: A guide for gardeners, Fiona Matthews (Osmia Publications, 2004)
Collins Field Guide to the Mammals of Britain and Europe, David Macdonald and Priscilla Barrett (Collins, 1993)

Mosses, liverworts and ferns
Grasses, Ferns, Mosses and Lichens of Great Britain and Ireland, Roger Phillips and Sheila Grant (Pan, 1980)
Moss Gardening, George Schenk (Timber Press, 1997)
New Naturalist: Mosses and Liverworts, Ron Porley (Collins, 2005)

Reptiles and amphibians
Collins Field Guide to the Reptiles and Amphibians of Britain and Europe, Nick Arnold and Denys Ovenden (Collins, 2002)

Trees
Collins Tree Guide, Owen Johnson (Collins, 2006)
Collins Wild Guide: Trees, Bob Press (Collins, 2005)
New Naturalist: Woodlands, Oliver Rackham (Collins, 2006)
The Secret Life of Trees, Colin Tudge (Penguin, 2006)

Wildflowers
Complete British Wild Flowers, Paul Sterry (Collins, 2006)
Field Guide to the Wild Flowers of Britain (Reader's Digest, 2001)
Flora Britannica, Richard Mabey (Chatto & Windus, 1996)

WILDLIFE GARDENING

Bird-Friendly Garden, The, Stephen Moss (Collins, 2004)

Collins Practical Gardener: Wild Gardens, Jenny Hendy (Collins, 2005)

New Naturalist: Garden Natural History, Stefan Buczacki (Collins, 2007)

How to Attract Butterflies to Your Garden, John and Maureen Tampion (Guild of Master Craftsmen, 2003)

How to Make A Wildlife Garden, Chris Baines (Frances Lincoln, 2000)

No Nettles Required: The Reassuring Truth About Wildlife Gardening, Ken Thompson (Eden Books, 2006)

RSPB Birdfeeder Guide, Robert Burton and Peter Holden (Dorling Kindersley, 2003)

Wildlife-Friendly Garden, The, Michael Chinery (Collins, 2006)

Wildlife Friendly Plants, Rosemary Creeser (Collins & Brown, 2004)

Wildlife Gardening for Everyone, Malcolm Tait (Think Publishing, 2006)

GENERAL GARDENING

Allotment Book, The, Andi Clevely (Collins, 2006)

Collins Complete Garden Manual, Adam Pasco (Collins, 2004)

Commonsense Gardener, The, Stefan Buczacki (Frances Lincoln, 2004)

Gardening with Children, Kim Wilde (Collins, 2007)

Plant Solutions, Nigel Colborn (Collins, 2006)

Pests, Diseases and Disorders of Garden Plants, Stefan Buczacki and Keith Harris (Collins, 2005)

RHS Encyclopedia of Gardening, Christopher Brickell (Editor in Chief) (Dorling Kindersley, 2002)

RHS Encyclopedia of Perennials, Graham Rice (Dorling Kindersley, 2006)

RHS Encyclopedia of Plants and Flowers, Christopher Brickell (Dorling Kindersley, 2006)

RHS Pests and Diseases, Pippa Greenwood and Andrew Halstead (Dorling Kindersley, 2003)

Young Gardener, Stefan and Beverley Buczacki (Frances Lincoln, 2006)

COMPOSTING AND ORGANIC PRACTICE

Compost, Clare Foster (Cassell, 2005)

Create Compost, Pauline Pears (Impact Publishing, 2004)

HDRA: Encyclopedia of Organic Gardening, Pauline Pears (Editor) (Dorling Kindersley, 2005)

How to Make Soil and Save Earth, Allan Shepherd (CAT Publications, 2003)

Little Book of Garden Heroes, The, Allan Shepherd (CAT Publications, 2004)

Organic Gardening, Geoff Hamilton (Dorling Kindersley, 2004)

Weeds: Friend or Foe?, Sally Roth (Carroll and Brown, 2001)

PONDS

Collins Practical Gardener: Water Gardening, Graham Clarke (Collins, 2004)

Pond Specialist, The, Alan and Gill Bridgewater (New Holland, 2004)

Wildlife Pond Handbook, The, Louise Bardsley (New Holland, 2003)

GARDEN SCIENCE AND CONSERVATION

An Ear to the Ground: Garden Science for Ordinary Mortals, Ken Thompson (Eden Books, 2003)

Biodiversity: A Beginner's Guide, John Spicer (Oneworld Publications, 2006)

Ecology for Gardeners, Carroll and Salt (Timber Press, 2004)

Ground Rules for Gardeners, Stefan Buczacki (Collins, 1986)

Habitat Creation and Repair, O.L. Gilbert and Penny Anderson (Oxford University Press, 1998)

Managing Habitats for Conservation, William Sutherland and David Hill (Cambridge University Press, 2005)

Silent Spring, Rachel Carson (Penguin, 2000)

Understanding your Garden, Stefan Buczacki (Cambridge University Press, 1990)

Resources

GARDENING ORGANISATIONS
Garden Organic (HDRA)
Ryton Organic Gardens,
Coventry, Warwickshire,
CV8 3LG
+44 (0)24 7630 3517
enquiry@hdra.org.uk
www.gardenorganic.org.uk

National Council for the Conservation of Plants and Gardens (NCCPG)
The Stable Courtyard, Wisley Garden,
Wisley, Woking, Surrey, GU23 6QP
+44 (0)1483 211 465
info@nccpg.org.uk
www.nccpg.com

National Society of Allotment and Leisure Gardeners Ltd
O'Dell House, Hunters Road,
Corby, Northamptonshire,
NN17 5JE
+44 (0)1536 266 576
natsoc@nsalg.org.uk
www.nsalg.org.uk

Royal Botanic Gardens, Edinburgh
20A Inverleith Row,
Edinburgh, EH3 5LR
+44 (0)131 552 717
www.rbge.org.uk

Royal Botanic Gardens, Kew
Richmond, Surrey, TW9 3AB
+44 (0)20 8332 5655
info@kew.org
www.rbgkew.org.uk

Royal Horticultural Society (RHS)
80 Vincent Square,
London, SW1P 2PE
+44 (0)845 260 5000
info@rhs.org.uk
www.rhs.org.uk

WILDLIFE AND CONSERVATION ORGANISATIONS

The Amateur Entomologists' Society (insects)
PO Box 8774, London, SW7 5ZG
contact@amentsoc.org
www.amentsoc.org

Bat Conservation Trust
Unit 2, 15 Cloisters House,
8 Battersea Park Road,
London, SW8 4BG
+44 (0)20 7627 2629
enquiries@bats.org.uk
www.bats.org.uk

Bees, Wasps and Ants Recording Society (BWARS)
5 St. Edward's Close, East Grinstead,
West Sussex, RH19 1JP
+44 (0)1342 325 387
bwars@insectpix.net
www.bwars.com

Botanical Society of the British Isles
Botany Department, The Natural
History Museum, Cromwell Road,
London, SW7 5BD
alex@whildassociates.co.uk
www.bsbi.org.uk

British Arachnological Society
(spiders)
100 Hayling Avenue, Little Paxton,
St. Neots, Cambridgeshire, PE19 6HQ
+44 (0)1480 471 064
info@ britishspiders.org.uk
www.britishspiders.org.uk

British Dragonfly Society
23 Bowker Way, Whittlesey,
Peterborough, Cambridgeshire,
PE7 1PY
bdssecretary@dragonflysoc.org.uk
www.dragonflysoc.org.uk

British Entomological and Natural History Society (insects)
c/o The Pelham-Clinton Building,
Dinton Pastures Country Park,
Davis Street, Hurst, Reading,
Berkshire, RG10 0TH
enquiries@benhs.org.uk
www.benhs.org.uk

The British Hedgehog Preservation Society (BHPS)
Hedgehog House, Dhustone,
Ludlow, Shropshire, SY8 3PL
+44 (0)1584 890 801
info@britishhedgehogs.org.uk
www.britishhedgehogs.org.uk

British Mycological Society (fungi)
The Wolfson Wing, Jodrell
Laboratory, Royal Botanic Gardens,
Kew, Richmond, Surrey, TW9 3AB
info@britmycolsoc.org.uk
www.britmycolsoc.org.uk

British Naturalists' Association
P.O. Box 5682, Corby,
Northamptonshire, NN17 2ZW
+44 (0)1536 262 977
info@bna-naturalists.org
www.bna-naturalists.org

British Trust for Conservation Volunteers (BTCV)
Sedum House, Mallard Way
Potteric Carr, Doncaster,
South Yorkshire, DN4 8DB

+44 (0)1302 388 888
information@btcv.org.uk
www.2.btcv.org.uk

British Trust for Ornithology (BTO)
The Nunnery, Thetford,
Norfolk, IP24 2PU
+44 (0)1842 750 050
info@bto.org
www.bto.org

Buglife - The Invertebrate Conservation Trust
170A Park Road, Peterborough,
Cambridgeshire, PE1 2UF
+44 (0)1733 201 210
info@buglife.org.uk
www.buglife.org.uk

Butterfly Conservation
Manor Yard, East Lulworth,
Wareham, Dorset, BH20 5QP
+44 (0)870 774 430
info@butterfly-conservation.org
www.butterfly-conservation.org

English Nature
Northminster House, Peterborough,
Cambridgeshire, PE1 1UA
+44 (0)1733 455 000
enquiries@english-nature.org.uk
www.english-nature.org.uk

The Entomological Livestock Group (suppliers of insects)
11 Rock Gardens, Aldershot,
Hampshire, GU11 3AD
pwbelg@clara.co.uk
www.pwbelg.clara.net

Froglife
White Lodge, London Road,
Peterborough, Cambridgeshire,
PE7 0LG
+44 (0)1733 558 844
info@froglife.org
www.froglife.org

The Hawk and Owl Trust
PO Box 100, Taunton,
Somerset, TA4 2WX

+44 (0)870 990 3889
enquiries@hawkandowl.org
www.hawkandowl.org

The Herpetological Conservation Trust (amphibians and reptiles)
655A Christchurch Road, Boscombe, Bournemouth, Dorset, BH1 4AP
+44 (0)1202 391 319
www.herpconstrust.org.uk

Joint Nature Conservation Committee (JNCC)
Monkstone House, City Road, Peterborough, Cambridgeshire, PE1 1JY
+44 (0)1733 562 626
comment@jncc.gov.uk
www.jncc.gov.uk

The Mammal Society
2B Inworth Street, London, SW11 3EP
+44 (0)20 7350 2200
enquiries@mammal.org.uk
www.abdn.ac.uk/mammal

Mammals Trust UK
15 Cloisters House, 8 Battersea Park Road, London, SW8 4BG
+44 (0)20 7498 5262
enquiries@mtuk.org
www.mtuk.org

The National Trust
PO Box 39, Warrington, Cheshire, WA5 7WD
+44 (0)870 458 400
enquiries@thenationaltrust.org.uk
www.nationaltrust.org.uk

Pond Conservation
School of Life Sciences, Oxford Brookes University, Gipsy Lane, Headington, Oxford, Oxfordshire, OX3 0BP
+44 (0)1865 483 249
info@pondconservation.org.uk
www.pondstrust.org.uk

Plantlife International
The Wild-Plant Conservation Charity
14 Rollestone Street, Salisbury, Wiltshire, SP1 1DX
+44 (0)1722 342 730
enquiries@plantlife.org.uk
www.plantlife.org.uk

Royal Entomological Society
(insects)
41 Queen's Gate, London, SW7 5HR
+44 (0)20 7584 8361
www.royensoc.co.uk

Royal Society for the Protection of Birds (RSPB)
The Lodge, Sandy, Bedfordshire, SG19 2DL
+44 (0)1767 680 551
www.rspb.org.uk

The Tree Council
71 Newcomen Street, London, SE1 1YT
+44 (0)20 7407 9992
Info@treecouncil.org.uk
www.treecouncil.org.uk

The Wild Flower Society
82A High Street, Sawston,

Cambridge, Cambridgeshire, CB2 4HJ
+44 (0)1223 830 665
wfs@grantais.demon.co.uk
www.thewildflowersociety.com

Wildfowl & Wetlands Trust
Slimbridge, Gloucestershire, GL2 7BT
+44 (0)1453 891 900
enquiries@wwt.org.uk
www.wwt.org.uk

The Wildlife Trusts
The Kiln, Waterside, Mather Road, Newark, Nottinghamshire, NG24 1WT
+44 (0)870 036 7711
enquiry@wildlifetrusts.org
www.wildlifetrusts.org

Wildlife Watch (environmental action club for kids)
The Wildlife Trusts, The Kiln, Waterside, Mather Road Newark, Nottinghamshire, NG24 1WT
+44 (0)870 036 7711
watch@wildlifetrusts.org
www.wildlifewatch.org.uk

The Woodland Trust
Autumn Park, Dysart Road Grantham, Lincolnshire, NG31 6LL
+44 (0)1476 581 111
www.woodland-trust.org.uk

WWF – the global environment network
Panda House, Weyside Park, Godalming, Surrey, GU7 1XR
+44 (0)1483 426 444
www.wwf.org.uk

Index

Figures in italics indicate captions.

Picture credits

All pictures copyright Stefan Buczacki except those listed below

9 © Harper Collins: Nikki English. **6** © Mike Newton. **8** © Harper Collins. **10** © Airedale Publishing: David Murphy. **11** © NHPA: Mike Lane. **13** © Dorling Kindersley. **15** © Harper Collins. **16** © Harper Collins. **17** © NHPA: Manfred Danegger. **19** © NHPA:Laurie Campbell. **20** © NHPA: Ernie Janes. **22[l]** © Harper Collins. **22[r]** © NHPA: Mike Lane. **24** © Harper Collins. **25[l]** © NHPA: Alan Barnes. **26** © Dorling Kindersley: Kim Taylor. **27** © Harper Collins. **28** © Airedale Publishing: Sarah Cuttle. **29** © Harper Collins: Nikki English. **30** © NHPA: Stephen Dalton. **31[tr, cl, bl]** © Airedale Publishing: David Murphy. **32** © Harper Collins. **33** © NHPA: Stephen Dalton. **35** © Airedale Publishing: Mike Newton. **37** © Harper Collins. **39[t]** © NHPA: Laurie Campbell. **41** © Airedale Publishing: Sarah Cuttle. **42** © Airedale Publishing: Sarah Cuttle. **44** © Airedale Publishing: Sarah Cuttle. **45** © Airedale Publishing: David Murphy. **46** © Dorling Kindersley: David Tipling. **49** © Murdo Culver. **52** © Airedale Publishing: Sarah Cuttle. **54** © Airedale Publishing: David Murphy. **55** © NHPA: Ernie Janes. **58** © NHPA: Stephen Dalton. **59** © NHPA: Stephen Dalton. **60** © Airedale Publishing: Ruth Prentice. **61** © NHPA: Ernie Janes. **63** © NHPA: Stephen Dalton. **65** © NHPA: Joe Blossom. **66** © Dorling Kindersley: Frank Greenaway. **67[tr]** © Airedale Publishing: David Murphy. **67[bl]** © NHPA: Stephen Dalton. **68** © Airedale Publishing: Sarah Cuttle. **70[tl]** © Harper Collins: Nikki English. **71[b]** © Airedale Publishing: Ruth Prentice. **72** © Harper Collins: Nikki English. **74** © NHPA: Laurie Campbell. **79[l.c,r]** © Airedale Publishing: David Murphy. **80** © Airedale Publishing: David Murphy. **87** © Airedale Publishing: David Murphy. **88** © Harper Collins: Nikki English. **89** © Mike Newton. **90[br]** © Harper Collins. **93[tr, tl, bl, br]** © Harper Collins. **95[tl, tr, bl, br]** © Harper Collins. **96[r]** © Airedale Publishing: Sarah Cuttle. **97[tl, tr]** © Airedale Publishing: David Murphy. **97[br]** © Dorling Kindersley. **99** © Harper Collins: Nikki English. **101** © Airedale Publishing: Mike Newton. **103[l]** © Dorling Kindersley. **103[r]** © Harper Collins. **105** © Murdo Culver.

106[r] © Murdo Culver. **107** © Murdo Culver. **108[l, r]** © Harper Collins: Nikki English. **109** © Harper Collins: Christian Barnett. **110** © Airedale Publishing: Sarah Cuttle. **112** © Harper Collins: Christian Barnett. **115[bl, r]** © Airedale Publishing: Sarah Cuttle. **116[r]** © Airedale Publishing: Sarah Cuttle. **117** © Airedale Publishing: Sarah Cuttle. **119** © Mike Newton. **120** © Dorling Kindersley. **123[tr, bl]** © Harper Collins. **124[tr, tl]** © Harper Collins. **127** © Murdo Culver. **130** © Harper Collins. **132** © NHPA: Andy Rouse. **134[l]** © Harper Collins. **134[r]** © NHPA: Mike Lane. **135** © NHPA: Stephen Dalton. **137** © Harper Collins: Nikki English. **139[tr]** © Harper Collins. **139[bl]** © Harper Collins: Nikki English. **139[bc, br]** © Airedale Publishing. **142** © Airedale Publishing: Ruth Prentice. **143** © Airedale Publishing: Sarah Cuttle. **144[l]** © Harper Collins: Christian Barnett. **144-5** © Mike Newton. **146** © Airedale Publishing: David Murphy. **149** © Mike Newton. **151[tr, br]** © Harper Collins. **153** © Airedale Publishing: David Murphy. **154** © Mike Newton. **155[t]** © Airedale Publishing: David Murphy. **155[b]** © Airedale Publishing: David Murphy. **159[t]** © Harper Collins. **160[l]** © Pictorial Meadows/ www.pictorialmeadows.co.uk. **160-1** © Mike Newton. **167** © Airedale Publishing: David Murphy. **169[b]** © Harper Collins. **170** © NHPA: Alan Barnes. **171** © Paul Hackney/www.habitas.org.uk/flora. **173[t]** © Harper Collins: Nikki English. **173[b]** © NHPA: Simon Booth. **174-5** © Mike Newton. **176** © NHPA: Ernie Janes. **178[l]** © Harper Collins: Christian Barnett. **178[r]** © Mike Newton. **179** © Murdo Culver. **184** © Dorling Kindersley: Jonathan Buckley. **189[cr, br]** © Harper Collins. **191** © NHPA: Roy Waller. **192** © Airedale Publishing: David Murphy. **194** © Airedale Publishing: Sarah Cuttle. **197** © Airedale Publishing: Sarah Cuttle. **198[r]** © Airedale Publishing: Sarah Cuttle. **199** © Airedale Publishing: David Murphy. **202** © Airedale Publishing: Sarah Cuttle. **203** © Airedale Publishing: Sarah Cuttle. **204[tl]** © Airedale Publishing: David Murphy. **204[tr, b]** © Airedale Publishing: Sarah Cuttle. **205** © Airedale Publishing: David Murphy. **206[l]** © Airedale Publishing: David Murphy. **206[r]** © Harper Collins: Christian Barnett. **207** © Airedale Publishing: Sarah Cuttle. **208** © Harper Collins: Christian Barnett.